OTHER PLAYS BY DAVID RABE

The Basic Training of Pavlo Hummel
Sticks and Bones
The Orphan
In the Boom Boom Room

STREAMERS

STREAMERS
DAVID RABE

ALFRED A. KNOPF • NEW YORK • 1988

Photographs by courtesy of Martha Swope

Library of Congress Cataloging in Publication Data
Rabe, David.   Streamers.
I. Title.
PS3568.A23S85   1977   812'.5'4   76-44000
ISBN 0-394-41120-X
ISBN 0-394-73314-2 pbk.

Grateful acknowledgment is made to Grove Press, Inc., for permission to reprint an excerpt from "Master Ssu, Master Yü, Master Li and Master Lai" (Chuang-Tzu). Reprinted from *Anthology of Chinese Literature*, edited by Cyril Birch. Copyright © 1965 by Grove Press, Inc.

Manufactured in the United States of America
Eighth printing, April 1988

For **MIKE NICHOLS**

and **WYLIE WALKER**

MASTER SSU, MASTER YÜ, MASTER LI AND MASTER LAI

All at once Master Yü fell ill, and Master Ssu went to ask how he was. "Amazing!" exclaimed Master Yü. "Look, the Creator is making me all crookedy! My back sticks up like a hunchback's so that my vital organs are on top of me. My chin is hidden down around my navel, my shoulders are up above my head, and my pigtail points at the sky. It must be due to some dislocation of the forces of the yin and the yang...."

"Do you resent it?" asked Master Ssu.

"Why, no," replied Master Yü. "What is there to resent...?"

Then suddenly Master Lai also fell ill. Gasping for breath, he lay at the point of death. His wife and children gathered round in a circle and wept. Master Li, who had come to find out how he was, said to them, "Shoooooo! Get back! Don't disturb the process of change."

And he leaned against the doorway and chatted with Master Lai. "How marvelous the Creator is!" he exclaimed. "What is he going to make out of you next? Where is he going to send you? Will he make you into a rat's liver? Will he make you into a bug's arm?"

"A child obeys his father and mother and goes wherever he is told, east or west, south or north," said Master Lai. "And the yin and the yang—how much more are they to a man than father or mother! Now that they have brought me to the verge of death, how perverse it would be of me to refuse to obey them.... So now I think of heaven and earth as a great furnace and the Creator as a skilled smith. What place could he send me that would not be all right? I will go off peacefully to sleep, and then with a start I will wake up."

—CHUANG-TZU

They so mean around here, they steal your sweat.

—SONNY LISTON

STREAMERS was produced by the Long Wharf Theater on January 30, 1976, under the direction of Mike Nichols, with the following cast:

MARTIN	Michael-Raymond O'Keefe
RICHIE	Peter Evans
CARLYLE	Joe Fields
BILLY	John Heard
ROGER	Herbert Jefferson, Jr.
COKES	Dolph Sweet
ROONEY	Kenneth McMillan
M.P. LIEUTENANT	Stephen Mendillo
PFC HINSON (M.P.)	Ron Siebert
PFC CLARK (M.P.)	Michael Kell

Produced by the Long Wharf Theater; set by Tony Walton; costumes by Bill Walker; lighting by Ronald Wallace; stage manager, Nina Seely.

STREAMERS *was produced in New York by Joseph Papp on April 21, 1976, at the Mitzi Newhouse Theater, Lincoln Center, under the direction of Mike Nichols, with the following cast:*

MARTIN	Michael Kell
RICHIE	Peter Evans
CARLYLE	Dorian Harewood
BILLY	Paul Rudd
ROGER	Terry Alexander
COKES	Dolph Sweet
ROONEY	Kenneth McMillan
M.P. LIEUTENANT	Arlen Dean Snyder
PFC HINSON (M.P.)	Les Roberts
PFC CLARK (M.P.)	Mark Metcalf
FOURTH M.P.	Miklos Horvath

Associate producer, Bernard Gersten; set by Tony Walton; costumes by Bill Walker; lighting by Ronald Wallace; stage manager, Nina Seely.

STREAMERS

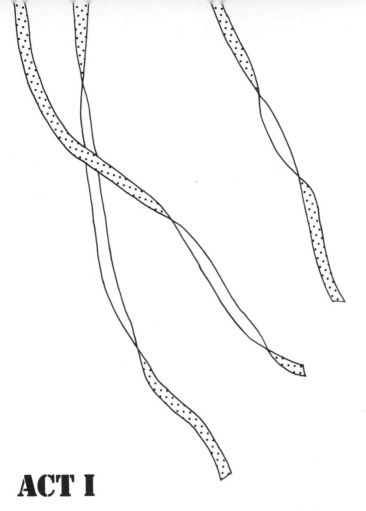

ACT I

The set is a large cadre room thrusting angularly toward the audience. The floor is wooden and brown. Brightly waxed in places, it is worn and dull in other sections. The back wall is brown and angled. There are two lights at the center of the ceiling. They hang covered by green metal shades. Against the back wall and to the stage right side are three wall lockers, side by side. Stage center in the back wall is the door, the only entrance to the room. It opens onto a hallway that runs off to the latrines, showers, other cadre rooms and larger barracks rooms. There are three bunks. BILLY'S bunk is parallel to ROGER'S bunk. They are upstage and on either side of the room, and face downstage. RICHIE's bunk is downstage and at a right angle to BILLY's bunk. At the foot of each bunk is a green wooden footlocker. There is a floor outlet near ROGER's bunk. He uses it for his radio. A reading lamp is clamped on to the metal piping at the head of RICHIE's bunk. A wooden chair stands beside the wall lockers. Two mops hang in the stage left corner near a trash can.

It is dusk as the lights rise on the room. RICHIE is seated and bowed forward wearily on his bunk. He wears his long-sleeved khaki summer dress uniform. Upstage behind him is MARTIN, a thin, dark young man, pacing, worried. A white towel stained red with blood is wrapped around his wrist. He paces several steps and falters, stops. He stands there.

RICHIE Honest to God, Martin, I don't know what to say anymore. I don't know what to tell you.

MARTIN *(Beginning to pace again)* I mean it. I just can't stand it. Look at me.

RICHIE I know.

MARTIN I hate it.

RICHIE We've got to make up a story. They'll ask you a hundred questions.

MARTIN Do you know how I hate it?

RICHIE Everybody does. Don't you think I hate it, too?

MARTIN I enlisted, though. I enlisted and I hate it.

RICHIE I enlisted, too.

MARTIN I vomit every morning. I get the dry heaves. In the middle of every night.
(He flops down on the corner of BILLY's bed and sits there, slumped forward, shaking his head.)

RICHIE You can stop that. You can.

MARTIN No.

RICHIE You're just scared. It's just fear.

MARTIN They're all so mean; they're all so awful. I've got two years to go. Just thinking about it is going to make me sick. I thought it would be different from the way it is.

RICHIE But you could have died, for God's sake.
(*RICHIE has turned now; he is facing MARTIN.*)

MARTIN I just wanted out.

RICHIE I might not have found you, though. I might not have come up here.

MARTIN I don't care. I'd be out.
(*The door opens and a black man in filthy fatigues—they are grease-stained and dark with sweat—stands there. He is CARLYLE, looking about. RICHIE, seeing him, rises and moves toward him.*)

RICHIE No. Roger isn't here right now.

CARLYLE Who isn't?

RICHIE He isn't here.

CARLYLE They tole me a black boy livin' in here. I don't see him.
(*He looks suspiciously about the room.*)

RICHIE That's what I'm saying. He isn't here. He'll be back later. You can come back later. His name is Roger.

MARTIN I slit my wrist.
(*Thrusting out the bloody, towel-wrapped wrist toward CARLYLE.*)

RICHIE Martin! Jesus!

MARTIN I did.

RICHIE He's kidding. He's kidding.

CARLYLE What was his name? Martin?
(*CARLYLE is confused and the confusion has made him angry. He moves toward MARTIN.*)
You Martin?

MARTIN Yes.
(*As BILLY, a white in his mid-twenties, blond and trim, appears in the door, whistling, carrying a slice of pie on a paper napkin. Sensing something, he falters, looks at CARLYLE, then RICHIE.*)

BILLY Hey, what's goin' on?

CARLYLE (*Turning, leaving*) Nothin', man. Not a thing.
(*BILLY looks questioningly at RICHIE. Then, after placing the piece of pie on the chair beside the door, he crosses to his footlocker.*)

RICHIE He came in looking for Roger, but he didn't even know his name.

BILLY (*Sitting on his footlocker, he starts taking off his shoes.*) How come you weren't at dinner, Rich? I brought you a piece of pie. Hey, Martin.
(*MARTIN thrusts out his towel-wrapped wrist.*)

MARTIN I cut my wrist, Billy.

RICHIE Oh, for God's sake, Martin!
(*He whirls away.*)

BILLY Huh?

MARTIN I did.

RICHIE You are disgusting, Martin.

MARTIN No. It's the truth. I did. I am not disgusting.

RICHIE Well, maybe it isn't disgusting, but it certainly is disappointing.

BILLY What are you guys talking about?
(*Sitting there, he really doesn't know what is going on.*)

MARTIN I cut my wrists, I slashed them, and Richie is pretending I didn't.

RICHIE I am not. And you only cut one wrist and you didn't slash it.

MARTIN I can't stand the army anymore, Billy.
(*He is moving now to petition* BILLY, *and* RICHIE *steps between them.*)

RICHIE Billy, listen to me. This is between Martin and me.

MARTIN It's between me and the army, Richie.

RICHIE (*Taking* MARTIN *by the shoulders as* BILLY *is now trying to get near* MARTIN) Let's just go outside and talk, Martin. You don't know what you're saying.

BILLY Can I see? I mean, did he really do it?

RICHIE No!

MARTIN I did.

BILLY That's awful. Jesus. Maybe you should go to the infirmary.

RICHIE I washed it with peroxide. It's not deep. Just let us be. Please. He just needs to straighten out his thinking a little, that's all.

BILLY Well, maybe I could help him?

MARTIN Maybe he could.

RICHIE *(Suddenly pushing at* **MARTIN**. **RICHIE** *is angry and exasperated. He wants* **MARTIN** *out of the room.)* Get out of here, Martin. Billy, you do some push-ups or something.
(Having been pushed toward the door, **MARTIN** *wanders out.)*

BILLY No.

RICHIE I know what Martin needs.
*(***RICHIE** *whirls and rushes into the hall after* **MARTIN**, *leaving* **BILLY** *scrambling to get his shoes on.)*

BILLY You're no doctor, are you? I just want to make sure he doesn't have to go to the infirmary, then I'll leave you alone.
(One shoe on, he grabs up the second and runs out the door into the hall after them.)
Martin! Martin, wait up!
(Silence. The door has been left open. Fifteen or twenty seconds pass. Then someone is heard coming down the hall. He is singing "Get a Job" and trying to do the voices and harmonies of a vocal group. **ROGER**, *a tall, well-built black in long-sleeved khakis, comes in the door. He has a laundry bag over his shoulder, a pair of clean civilian trousers and a shirt on a hanger in his other hand. After dropping the bag on his bed, he goes to his wall locker, where he carefully hangs up the civilian clothes. Returning to the bed, he picks up the laundry and then, as if struck, he throws the bag down on the bed, tears off his tie and sits down angrily on the bed. For a moment, with his head in his hands, he sits there. Then, resolutely, he rises, takes up the position of attention, and simply topples forward, his hands leaping out to break his fall at the*

last instant and put him into the push-up position. Counting in a hissing, whispering voice, he does ten push-ups before giving up and flopping onto his belly. He simply doesn't have the will to do any more. Lying there, he counts rapidly on.)

ROGER Fourteen, fifteen. Twenty. Twenty-five.

*(*BILLY,** shuffling dejectedly back in, sees* **ROGER** *lying there.* **ROGER** *springs to his feet, heads toward his footlocker, out of which he takes an ashtray and a pack of cigarettes.)*
You come in this area, you come in here marchin', boy: standin' tall.

*(*BILLY,** having gone to his wall locker, is tossing a Playboy magazine onto his bunk. He will also remove a towel, a Dopp kit and a can of foot powder.)*

BILLY I was marchin'.

ROGER You call that marchin'?

BILLY I was as tall as I am; I was marchin'—what do you want?

ROGER Outa here, man; outa this goddamn typin'-terrors outfit and into some kinda real army. Or else out and free.

BILLY So go; who's stoppin' you; get out. Go on.

ROGER Ain't you a bitch.

BILLY You and me more regular army than the goddamn sergeants around this place, you know that?

ROGER I was you, Billy boy, I wouldn't be talkin' so sacrilegious so loud, or they be doin' you like they did the ol sarge.

BILLY He'll get off.

ROGER Sheee-it, he'll get off.

> (Sitting down on the side of his bed and facing BILLY, ROGER lights up a cigarette. BILLY has arranged the towel, Dopp kit and foot powder on his own bed.)

Don't you think L.B.J. want to have some sergeants in that Vietnam, man? In Disneyland, baby? Lord have mercy on the ole sarge. He goin' over there to be Mickey Mouse.

BILLY Do him a lot of good. Make a man outa him.

ROGER That's right, that's right. He said the same damn thing about himself and you, too, I do believe. You know what's the ole boy's MOS? His Military Occupation Specialty? Demolitions, baby. Expert is his name.

BILLY (Taking off his shoes and beginning to work on a sore toe, BILLY hardly looks up.) You're kiddin' me.

ROGER Do I jive?

BILLY You mean that poor ole bastard who cannot light his own cigar for shakin' is supposed to go over there blowin' up bridges and shit? Do they wanna win this war or not, man?

ROGER Ole sarge was over in Europe in the big one, Billy. Did all kinds a bad things.

BILLY (Swinging his feet up onto the bed, BILLY sits, cutting the cuticles on his toes, powdering his feet.) Was he drinkin' since he got the word?

ROGER Was he breathin', Billy? Was he breathin'?

BILLY Well, at least he ain't cuttin' his fuckin' wrists.

> (Silence. ROGER looks at BILLY, who keeps on working.)

Man, that's the real damn army over there, ain't it? That

ain't shinin' your belt buckle and standin' tall. And we might end up in it, man.

(Silence. ROGER, *rising, begins to sort his laundry.)*
Roger . . . you ever ask yourself if you'd rather fight in a war where it was freezin' cold or one where there was awful snakes? You ever ask that question?

ROGER Can't say I ever did.

BILLY We used to ask it all the time. All the time. I mean, us kids sittin' out on the back porch tellin' ghost stories at night. 'Cause it was Korea time and the newspapers were fulla pictures of soldiers in snow with white frozen beards; they got these rags tied around their feet. And snakes. We hated snakes. Hated 'em. I mean, it's bad enough to be in the jungle duckin' bullets, but then you crawl right into a goddamn snake. That's awful. That's awful.

ROGER It don't sound none too good.

BILLY I got my draft notice, goddamn Vietnam didn't even exist. I mean, it existed, but not as in a war we might be in. I started crawlin' around the floor a this house where I was stayin' 'cause I'd dropped outa school, and I was goin' "Bang, bang," pretendin'. Jesus.

ROGER *(Continuing with his laundry, he tries to joke.)* My first goddamn formation in basic, Billy, this NCO's up there jammin' away about how some a us are goin' to be dyin' in the war. I'm sayin', "What war? What that crazy man talkin' about?"

BILLY Us, too. I couldn't believe it. I couldn't believe it. And now we got three people goin' from here.

ROGER Five.

(They look at each other, and then turn away, each returning to his task.)

BILLY It don't seem possible. I mean, people shootin' at you. Shootin' at you to kill you.
  (Slight pause)
It's somethin'.

ROGER What did you decide you preferred?

BILLY Huh?

ROGER Did you decide you would prefer the snakes or would you prefer the snow? 'Cause it look like it is going to be the snakes.

BILLY I think I had pretty much made my mind up on the snow.

ROGER Well, you just let 'em know that, Billy. Maybe they get one goin' special just for you up in Alaska. You can go to the Klondike. Fightin' some snowmen.
  *(**RICHIE** bounds into the room and shuts the door as if to keep out something dreadful. He looks at **ROGER** and **BILLY** and crosses to his wall locker, pulling off his tie as he moves. Tossing the tie into the locker, he begins unbuttoning the cuffs of his shirt.)*

RICHIE Hi, hi, hi, everybody. Billy, hello.

BILLY Hey.

ROGER What's happenin', Rich?
  *(Moving to the chair beside the door, **RICHIE** picks up the pie **BILLY** left there. He will place the pie atop the locker, and then, sitting, he will remove his shoes and socks.)*

RICHIE I simply did this rather wonderful thing for a friend of mine, helped him see himself in a clearer, more hopeful light—little room in his life for hope? And I feel very good. Didn't Billy tell you?

ROGER About what?

RICHIE About Martin.

ROGER No.

BILLY *(Looking up and speaking pointedly)* No.
(*RICHIE looks at* BILLY *and then at* ROGER. RICHIE *is truly confused.*)

RICHIE No? No?

BILLY What do I wanna gossip about Martin for?

RICHIE *(He really can't figure out what is going on with* BILLY. *Shoes and socks in hand, he heads for his wall locker.)* Who was planning to gossip? I mean, it did happen. We could talk about it. I mean, I wasn't hearing his goddamn confession. Oh, my sister told me Catholics were boring.

BILLY Good thing I ain't one anymore.

RICHIE *(Taking off his shirt, he moves toward* ROGER.*)* It really wasn't anything, Roger, except Martin made this rather desperate, pathetic gesture for attention that seems to have brought to the surface Billy's more humane and protective side.
(*Reaching out, he tousles* BILLY'S *hair.*)

BILLY Man, I am gonna have to obliterate you.

RICHIE *(Tossing his shirt into his locker)* I don't know what you're so embarrassed about.

BILLY I just think Martin's got enough trouble without me yappin' to everybody.
(*RICHIE has moved nearer* BILLY, *his manner playful and teasing.*)

RICHIE "Obliterate"? "Obliterate," did you say? Oh, Billy, you better say "shit," "ain't" and "motherfucker" real quick now or we'll all know just how far beyond the fourth grade you went.

ROGER *(Having moved to his locker, into which he is placing his folded clothes)* You hear about the ole sarge, Richard?

BILLY *(Grinning)* You ain't . . . shit . . . motherfucker.

ROGER *(Laughing)* All right.

RICHIE *(Moving center and beginning to remove his trousers)* Billy, no, no. Wit is my domain. You're in charge of sweat and running around the block.

ROGER You hear about the ole sarge?

RICHIE What about the ole sarge? Oh, who cares? Let's go to a movie. Billy, wanna? Let's go. C'mon.
(Trousers off, he hurries to his locker.)

BILLY Sure. What's playin'?

RICHIE I don't know. Can't remember. Something good, though.
(With a Playboy magazine he has taken from his locker, ROGER is settling down on his bunk, his back toward both BILLY and RICHIE.)

BILLY You wanna go, Rog?

RICHIE *(In mock irritation)* Don't ask Roger! How are we going to kiss and hug and stuff if he's there?

BILLY That ain't funny, man.
(He is stretched out on his bunk, and RICHIE comes bounding over to flop down and lie beside him.)

RICHIE And what time will you pick me up?

BILLY *(He pushes at* RICHIE, *knocking him off the bed and onto the floor.)* Well, you just fall down and wait, all right?

RICHIE Can I help it if I love you?
(Leaping to his feet, he will head to his locker, remove his shorts, put on a robe.)

ROGER You gonna take a shower, Richard?

RICHIE Cleanliness is nakedness, Roger.

ROGER Is that right? I didn't know that. Not too many people know that. You may be the only person in the world who know that.

RICHIE And godliness is in there somewhere, of course.
(Putting a towel around his neck, he is gathering toiletries to carry to the shower.)

ROGER You got your own way a lookin' at things, man. You cute.

RICHIE That's right.

ROGER You g'wan, have a good time in that shower.

RICHIE Oh, I will.

BILLY *(Without looking up from his feet, which he is powdering)* And don't drop your soap.

RICHIE I will if I want to.
(Already out the door, he slams it shut with a flourish.)

BILLY Can you imagine bein' in combat with Richie—people blastin' away at you—he'd probably want to hold your hand.

ROGER Ain't he somethin'?

BILLY Who's zat?

ROGER He's all right.

BILLY (*Rising, he heads toward his wall locker, where he will put the powder and Dopp kit.*) Sure he is, except he's livin' under water.

(*Looking at* **BILLY**, **ROGER** *senses something unnerving; it makes* **ROGER** *rise, and return his magazine to his footlocker.*)

ROGER I think we oughta do this area, man. I think we oughta do our area. Mop and buff this floor.

BILLY You really don't think he means that shit he talks, do you?

ROGER Huh? Awwww, man . . . Billy, no.

BILLY I'd put money on it, Roger, and I ain't got much money.

(**BILLY** *is trying to face* **ROGER** *with this, but* **ROGER**, *seated on his bed, has turned away. He is unbuttoning his shirt.*)

ROGER Man, no, no. I'm tellin' you, lad, you listen to the ole Rog. You seen that picture a that little dolly he's got in his locker? He ain't swish, man, believe me—he's cool.

BILLY It's just that ever since we been in this room, he's been different somehow. Somethin'.

ROGER No, he ain't.

(**BILLY** *turns to his bed, where he carefully starts folding the towel. Then he looks at* **ROGER**.)

BILLY You ever talk to any a these guys—queers, I mean? You ever sit down, just rap with one of 'em?

ROGER Hell, no; what I wanna do that for? Shit, no.

BILLY (*Crossing to the trash can in the corner, where he will shake the towel empty*) I mean, some of 'em are okay guys, just way up this bad alley, and you say to 'em, "I'm straight, be cool," they go their own way. But then there's these other ones, these bitches, man, and they're so crazy they think anybody can be had. Because they been had themselves. So you tell 'em you're straight and they just nod and smile. You ain't real to 'em. They can't see nothin' but themselves and these goddamn games they're always playin'.

(Having returned to his bunk, he is putting on his shoes.)
I mean, you can be decent about anything, Roger, you see what I'm sayin'? We're all just people, man, and some of us are hardly that. That's all I'm sayin'.

(There is a slight pause as he sits there thinking. Then he gets to his feet.)
I'll go get some buckets and stuff so we can clean up, okay? This area's a mess. This area ain't standin' tall.

ROGER That's good talk, lad; this area a midget you put it next to an area standin' tall.

BILLY Got to be good fuckin' troopers.

ROGER That's right, that's right. I know the meanin' of the words.

BILLY I mean, I just think we all got to be honest with each other—you understand me?

ROGER No, I don't understand you; one stupid fuckin' nigger like me—how's that gonna be?

BILLY That's right; mock me, man. That's what I need. I'll go get the wax.

(Out he goes, talking to himself and leaving the door open. For a moment ROGER *sits, thinking, and then he looks at* RICHIE'S *locker and gets to his feet and walks to the locker which he opens and looks at the pinup hang-*

ing on the inside of the door. He takes a step backward, looking.)

ROGER Sheee-it.
(Through the open door comes CARLYLE. ROGER doesn't see him. And CARLYLE stands there looking at ROGER and the picture in the locker.)

CARLYLE Boy . . . whose locker you lookin' into?

ROGER *(He is startled, but recovers.)* Hey, baby, what's happenin'?

CARLYLE That ain't your locker, is what I'm askin', nigger. I mean, you ain't got no white goddamn woman hangin' on your wall.

ROGER Oh, no—no, no.

CARLYLE You don't wanna be lyin' to me, 'cause I got to turn you in you lyin' and you do got the body a some white goddamn woman hangin' there for you to peek at nobody around but you—you can be thinkin' about that sweet wet pussy an' maybe it hot an' maybe it cool.

ROGER I could be thinkin' all that, except I know the penalty for lyin'.

CARLYLE Thank God for that.
(Extending his hand, palm up)

ROGER That's right. This here the locker of a faggot.
(And ROGER slaps CARLYLE's hand, palm to palm.)

CARLYLE Course it is; I see that; any damn body know that.
(ROGER crosses toward his bunk and CARLYLE swaggers about, pulling a pint of whiskey from his hip pocket.)
You want a shot? Have you a little taste, my man.

ROGER Naw.

CARLYLE C'mon. C'mon. I think you a Tom you don't drink outa my bottle.

(He thrusts the bottle toward ROGER and wipes a sweat- and grease-stained sleeve across his mouth.)

ROGER (Taking the bottle) Shit.

CARLYLE That right. How do I know? I just got in. New boy in town. Somewhere over there; I dunno. They dump me in amongst a whole bunch a pale, boring motherfuckers.

(CARLYLE is exploring the room. Finding BILLY's Playboy, he edges onto BILLY's bed and leafs nervously through the pages.)

I just come in from P Company, man, and I been all over this place, don't see too damn many of us. This outfit look like it a little short on soul. I been walkin' all around, I tell you, and the number is small. Like one hand you can tabu-late the lot of 'em. We got few brothers I been able to see, is what I'm sayin'. You and me and two cats down in the small bay. That's all I found.

(As ROGER is about to hand the bottle back, CARLYLE, al-most angrily, waves him off.)

No, no, you take another; take you a real taste.

ROGER It ain't so bad here. We do all right.

CARLYLE (He moves, shutting the door. Suspiciously, he ap-proaches ROGER.) How about the white guys? They give you any sweat? What's the situation? No jive. I like to know what is goin' on within the situation before that situation get a chance to be closin' in on me.

ROGER (Putting the bottle on the footlocker, he sits down.) Man, I'm tellin' you, it ain't bad. They're just pale, most of 'em, you know. They can't help it; how they gonna help it?

Some of 'em got little bit a soul, couple real good boys around this way. Get 'em little bit of Coppertone, they be straight, man.

CARLYLE How about the NCOs? We got any brother NCO watchin' out for us or they all white, like I goddamn well KNOW all the officers are? Fuckin' officers always white, man; fuckin' snow cones and bars everywhere you look.
(CARLYLE *cannot stay still. He moves to his right, his left; he sits, he stands.*)

ROGER First sergeant's a black man.

CARLYLE All right; good news. Hey, hey, you wanna go over the club with me, or maybe downtown? I got wheels. Let's be free.
(*Now he rushes at* ROGER.)
Let's be free.

ROGER Naw . . .

CARLYLE Ohhh, baby . . . !
(*He is wildly pulling at* ROGER *to get him to the door.*)

ROGER Some other time. I gotta get the area straight. Me and the guy sleeps in here too are gonna shape the place up a little.
(ROGER *has pulled free, and* CARLYLE *cannot understand. It hurts him, depresses him.*)

CARLYLE You got a sweet deal here an' you wanna keep it, that right?
(*He paces about the room, opens a footlocker, looks inside.*)
How you rate you get a room like this for yourself—you and a couple guys?

ROGER Spec 4. The three of us in here Spec 4.

CARLYLE You get a room then, huh?
(And suddenly, without warning or transition, he is angry.)
Oh, man, I hate this goddamn army. I hate this bastard army. I mean, I just got outa basic—off leave—you know? Back on the block for two weeks—and now here. They don't pull any a that petty shit, now, do they—that goddamn petty basic training bullshit? They do and I'm gonna be bustin' some head—my hand is gonna be upside all kinds a heads, 'cause I ain't gonna be able to endure it, man, not that kinda crap—understand?
(And again, he is rushing at ROGER.)
Hey, hey, oh, c'mon, let's get my wheels and make it, man, do me the favor.

ROGER How'm I gonna? I got my obligations.
(And CARLYLE spins away in anger.)

CARLYLE Jesus, baby, can't you remember the outside? How long it been since you been on leave? It is so sweet out there, nigger; you got it all forgot. I had such a sweet, sweet time. They doin' dances, baby, make you wanna cry. I hate this damn army.
(The anger overwhelms him.)
All these mother-actin' jacks givin' you jive about what you gotta do and what you can't do. I had a bad scene in basic —up the hill and down the hill; it ain't somethin' I enjoyed even a little. So they do me wrong here, Jim, they gonna be sorry. Some-damn-body! And this whole Vietnam THING— I do not dig it.
(He falls on his knees before ROGER. It is a gesture that begins as a joke, a mockery. And then a real fear pulses through him to nearly fill the pose he has taken.)

Lord, Lord, don't let 'em touch me. Christ, what will I do, they DO! Whoooooooooooooo! And they pullin' guys outa here, too, ain't they? Pullin' 'em like weeds, man; throwin' 'em into the fire. It's shit, man.

ROGER They got this ole sarge sleeps down the hall—just today they got him.

CARLYLE Which ole sarge?

ROGER He sleeps just down the hall. Little guy.

CARLYLE Wino, right?

ROGER Booze hound.

CARLYLE Yeh; I seen him. They got him, huh?

ROGER He's goin'; gotta be packin' his bags. And three other guys two days ago. And two guys last week.

CARLYLE *(Leaping up from* BILLY's *bed)* Ohhh, them bastards. And everybody just takes it. It ain't our war, brother. I'm tellin' you. That's what gets me, nigger. It ain't our war nohow because it ain't our country, and that's what burns my ass—that and everybody just sittin' and takin' it. They gonna be bustin' balls, man—kickin' and stompin'. Everybody here maybe one week from shippin' out to get blown clean away and, man, whata they doin'? They doin' what they told. That what they doin'. Like you? Shit! You gonna straighten up your goddamn area! Well, that ain't for me; I'm gettin' hat, and makin' it out where it's sweet and the people's livin'. I can't cut this jive here, man. I'm tellin' you. I can't cut it.
    (He has moved toward ROGER, *and behind him now* RICHIE *enters, running, his hair wet, traces of shaving cream on his face. Toweling his hair, he falters, seeing* CARLYLE. *Then he crosses to his locker.* CARLYLE *grins at*

ROGER, *looks at* RICHIE, *steps toward him and gives a little bow.)*
My name is Carlyle; what is yours?

RICHIE Richie.

CARLYLE *(He turns toward* ROGER *to share his joke.)* Hello. Where is Martin? That cute little Martin.
(And RICHIE *has just taken off his robe as* CARLYLE *turns back.)*
You cute, too, Richie.

RICHIE Martin doesn't live here.
(Hurriedly putting on underpants to cover his nakedness)

CARLYLE *(Watching* RICHIE, *he slowly turns toward* ROGER.)
You ain't gonna make it with me, man?

ROGER Naw . . . like I tole you. I'll catch you later.

CARLYLE That's sad, man; make me cry in my heart.

ROGER You g'wan get your head smokin'. Stop on back.

CARLYLE Okay, okay. Got to be one man one more time.
(On the move for the door, his hand extended palm up behind him, demanding the appropriate response)
Baby! Gimme! Gimme!
(Lunging, ROGER *slaps the hand.)*

ROGER G'wan home! G'wan home.

CARLYLE You gonna hear from me.
(And he is gone out the door and down the hallway.)

ROGER I can . . . and do . . . believe . . . that.
*(*RICHIE, *putting on his T-shirt, watches* ROGER, *who stubs out his cigarette, then crosses to the trash can to empty the ashtray.)*

RICHIE Who was that?

ROGER Man's new, Rich. Dunno his name more than that "Carlyle" he said. He's new—just outa basic.

RICHIE (*Powdering his thighs and under his arms*) Oh, my God . . .
   (*As* BILLY *enters, pushing a mop bucket with a wringer attached and carrying a container of wax*)

ROGER Me and Billy's gonna straighten up the area. You wanna help?

RICHIE Sure, sure; help, help.

BILLY (*Talking to* ROGER, *but turning to look at* RICHIE, *who is still putting powder under his arms*) I hadda steal the wax from Third Platoon.

ROGER Good man.

BILLY (*Moving to* RICHIE, *joking, yet really irritated in some strange way*) What? Whata you doin', singin'? Look at that, Rog. He's got enough jazz there for an entire beauty parlor. (*Grabbing the can from* RICHIE'S *hand*) What is this? Baby Powder! BABY POWDER!

RICHIE I get rashes.

BILLY Okay, okay, you get rashes, so what? They got powder for rashes that isn't baby powder.

RICHIE It doesn't work as good; I've tried it. Have you tried it? (*Grabbing* BILLY'S *waist,* RICHIE *pulls him close.* BILLY *knocks* RICHIE'S *hands away.*)

BILLY Man, I wish you could get yourself straight. I'll mop, too, Roger—okay? Then I'll put down the wax and you can spread it?
   (*He has walked away from* RICHIE.)

RICHIE What about buffing?

ROGER In the morning.
 (He is already busy mopping up near the door.)

RICHIE What do you want me to do?

BILLY *(Grabbing up a mop, he heads downstage to work.)* Get inside your locker and shut the door and don't holler for help. Nobody'll know you're there; you'll stay there.

RICHIE But I'm so pretty.

BILLY NOW!
 (Pointing to ROGER. *He wants to get this clear.)* Tell that man you mean what you're sayin', Richie.

RICHIE Mean what?

BILLY That you really think you're pretty.

RICHIE Of course I do; I am. Don't you think I am? Don't you think I am, Roger?

ROGER I tole you—you fulla shit and you cute, man. Carlyle just tole you you cute, too.

RICHIE Don't you think it's true, Billy?

BILLY It's like I tole you, Rog.

RICHIE What did you tell him?

BILLY That you go down; that you go up and down like a Yo-Yo and you go blowin' all the trees like the wind.
 *(*RICHIE *is stunned. He looks at* ROGER, *and then he turns and stares into his own locker. The others keep mopping.* RICHIE *takes out a towel, and putting it around his neck, he walks to where* BILLY *is working. He stands there, hurt, looking at* BILLY.*)*

RICHIE What the hell made you tell him I been down, Billy?

BILLY *(Still mopping)* It's in your eyes; I seen it.

RICHIE What?

BILLY You.

RICHIE What is it, Billy, you think you're trying to say? You and all your wit and intelligence—your *humanity*.

BILLY I said it, Rich; I said what I was tryin' to say.

RICHIE *Did* you?

BILLY I think I did.

RICHIE *Do* you?

BILLY Loud and clear, baby.
(Still mopping)

ROGER They got to put me in with the weirdos. Why is that, huh? How come the army *hate* me, do this shit to me—*know* what to do.
(Whimsical and then suddenly loud, angered, violent)
Now you guys put socks in your mouths, right now—get shut up—or I am gonna beat you to death with each other. Roger got work to do. To be doin' it!

RICHIE *(Turning to his bed, he kneels upon it.)* Roger, I think you're so innocent sometimes. Honestly, it's not such a terrible thing. Is it, Billy?

BILLY How would I know?
(He slams his mop into the bucket.)
Oh, go fuck yourself.

RICHIE Well, I can give it a try, if that's what you want. Can I think of you as I do?

BILLY *(Throwing down his mop)* GODDAMMIT! That's it! IT! *(He exits, rushing into the hall and slamming the door behind him.* ROGER *looks at* RICHIE. *Neither quite knows what is going on. Suddenly the door bursts open and* BILLY *storms straight over to* RICHIE, *who still kneels on the bed.)*
Now I am gonna level with you. Are you gonna listen? You gonna hear what I say, Rich, and not what you think I'm sayin'?
*(*RICHIE *turns away as if to rise, his manner flippant, disdainful.)*
No! Don't get cute; don't turn away cute. I wanna say somethin' straight out to you and I want you to hear it!

RICHIE I'm all ears, goddammit! For what, however, I do not know, except some boring evasion.

BILLY At least wait the hell till you hear me!

RICHIE *(In irritation)* Okay, okay! What?

BILLY Now this is level, Rich; this is straight talk.
(He is quiet, intense. This is difficult for him. He seeks the exactly appropriate words of explanation.)
No b.s. No tricks. What you do on the side, that's your business and I don't care about it. But if you don't cut the cute shit with me, I'm gonna turn you off. Completely. You ain't gonna get a good mornin' outa me, you understand, because it's gettin' bad around here. I mean, I know how you think—how you keep lookin' out and seein' yourself, and that's what I'm tryin' to tell you because that's all that's happenin', Rich. That's all there is to it when you look out at me and think there's some kind of approval or whatever you see in my eyes—you're just seein' yourself. And I'm talkin' the simple quiet truth to you, Rich. I swear I am.

(BILLY *looks away from* RICHIE *now and tries to go back to the mopping. It is embarrassing for them all.* ROGER *has watched, has tried to keep working.* RICHIE *has flopped back on his bunk. There is a silence.*)

RICHIE How . . . do . . . you want me to be? I don't know how else to be.

BILLY Ohhh, man, that ain't any part of it.
(*The mop is clenched in his hands.*)

RICHIE Well, I don't come from the same kind of world as you do.

BILLY Damn, Richie, you think Roger and I come off the same street?

ROGER Shit . . .

RICHIE All right. Okay. But I've just done what I wanted all of my life. If I wanted to do something, I just did it. Honestly. I've never had to work or anything like that and I've always had nice clothing and money for cab fare. Money for whatever I wanted. Always. I'm not like you are.

ROGER You ain't sayin' you really done that stuff, though, Rich.

RICHIE What?

ROGER That fag stuff.

RICHIE (*He continues looking at* ROGER *and then he looks away.*) Yes.

ROGER Do you even know what you're sayin', Richie? Do you even know what it means to be a fag?

RICHIE Roger, of course I know what it is. I just told you I've done it. I thought you black people were supposed to understand all about suffering and human strangeness. I thought

you had depth and vision from all your suffering. Has someone been misleading me? I just told you I did it. I know all
about it. Everything. All the various positions.

ROGER Yeh, so maybe you think you've tried it, but that don't
make you it. I mean, we used to . . . in the old neighborhood, man, we had a couple dudes swung that way. But
they was weird, man. There was this one little fella, he was
a screamin' goddamn faggot . . . uh . . .
   (He considers RICHIE, *wondering if perhaps he has of-
   fended him.)*
Ohhh, ohhh, you ain't no screamin' goddamn faggot,
Richie, no matter what you say. And the baddest man on
the block was my boy Jerry Lemon. So one day Jerry's got
the faggot in one a them ole deserted stairways and he's
bouncin' him off the walls. I'm just a little fella, see, and
I'm watchin' the baddest man on the block do his thing.
So he come bouncin' back into me instead of Jerry, and
just when he hit, he gave his ass this little twitch, man, like
he thought he was gonna turn me on. I'd never a thought
that was possible, man, for a man to be twitchin' his ass on
me, just like he thought he was a broad. Scared me to
death. I took off runnin'. Oh, oh, that ole neighborhood
put me into all kinds a crap. I did some sufferin', just like
Richie says. Like this once, I'm swingin' on up the street
after school, and outa this phone booth comes this man
with a goddamned knife stickin' outa his gut. So he sees
me and starts tryin' to pull his motherfuckin' coat out over
the handle, like he's worried about how he looks, man. "I
didn't know this was gonna happen," he says. And then he
falls over. He was just all of a sudden dead, man; just all of
a sudden dead. You ever seen anything like that, Billy? Any
crap like that?
   *(*BILLY, *sitting on* ROGER'S *bunk, is staring at* ROGER.*)*

BILLY You really seen that?

ROGER Richie's a big-city boy.

RICHIE Oh, no; never anything like that.

ROGER "Momma, help me," I am screamin'. "Jesus, Momma, help me." Little fella, he don't know how to act, he sees somethin' like that.
(*For a moment they are still, each thinking.*)

BILLY How long you think we got?

ROGER What do you mean?
(**ROGER** *is hanging up the mops;* **BILLY** *is now kneeling on* **ROGER'S** *bunk.*)

BILLY Till they pack us up, man, ship us out.

ROGER To the war, you mean? To Disneyland? Man, I dunno; that up to them IBM's. Them machines is figurin' that. Maybe tomorrow, maybe next week, maybe never.
(*The war—the threat of it—is the one thing they share.*)

RICHIE I was reading they're planning to build it all up to more than five hundred thousand men over there. Americans. And they're going to keep it that way until they win.

BILLY Be a great place to come back from, man, you know? I keep thinkin' about that. To have gone there, to have been there, to have seen it and lived.

ROGER (*Settling onto* **BILLY'S** *bunk, he lights a cigarette.*) Well, what we got right here is a fool, gonna probably be one a them five hundred thousand, too. Do you know I cry at the goddamn anthem yet sometimes? The flag is flyin' at a ball game, the ole Roger gets all wet in the eye. After all the shit been done to his black ass. But I don't know what I think about this war. I do not know.

BILLY I'm tellin' you, Rog—I've been doin' a lot a readin' and I think it's right we go. I mean, it's just like when North Korea invaded South Korea or when Hitler invaded Poland and all those other countries. He just kept testin' everybody and when nobody said no to him, he got so committed he couldn't back out even if he wanted. And that's what this Ho Chi Minh is doin'. And all these other Communists. If we let 'em know somebody is gonna stand up against 'em, they'll back off, just like Hitler would have.

ROGER There is folks, you know, who are sayin' L.B.J. is the Hitler, and not ole Ho Chi Minh at all.

RICHIE *(Talking as if this is the best news he's heard in years)* Well, I don't know anything at all about all that, but I am certain I don't want to go—whatever is going on. I mean, those Vietcong don't just shoot you and blow you up, you know. My God, they've got these other awful things they do: putting elephant shit on these stakes in the ground and then you step on 'em and you got elephant shit in a wound in your foot. The infection is horrendous. And then there's these caves they hide in and when you go in after 'em, they've got these snakes that they've tied by their tails to the ceiling. So it's dark and the snake is furious from having been hung by its tail and you crawl right into them—your face. My God.

BILLY They do not.
    (BILLY knows he has been caught; they all know it.)

RICHIE I read it, Billy. They do.

BILLY *(Completely facetious, yet the fear is real)* That's bull-shit, Richie.

ROGER That's right, Richie. They maybe do that stuff with the elephant shit, but nobody's gonna tie a snake by its tail, let ole Billy walk into it.

BILLY That's disgusting, man.

ROGER Guess you better get ready for the Klondike, my man.

BILLY That is probably the most disgusting thing I ever heard of. I DO NOT WANT TO GO! NOT TO NOWHERE WHERE THAT KINDA SHIT IS GOIN' ON! L.B.J. is Hitler; suddenly I see it all very clearly.

ROGER Billy got him a hatred for snakes.

RICHIE I hate them, too. They're hideous.

BILLY (*And now, as a kind of apology to* **RICHIE**, **BILLY** *continues his self-ridicule far into the extreme.*) I mean, that is one of the most awful things I ever heard of any person doing. I mean, any person who would hang a snake by its tail in the dark of a cave in the hope that some other person might crawl into it and get bitten to death, that first person is somebody who oughta be shot. And I hope the five hundred thousand other guys that get sent over there kill 'em all—all them gooks—get 'em all driven back into Germany, where they belong. And in the meantime, I'll be holding the northern border against the snowmen.

ROGER (*Rising from* **BILLY'S** *bed*) And in the meantime before that, we better be gettin' at the ole area here. Got to be strike troopers.

BILLY Right.

RICHIE Can I help?

ROGER Sure. Be good.
(*And* **ROGER** *crosses to his footlocker and takes out a radio.*)
Think maybe I put on a little music, though it's gettin' late. We got time. Billy, you think?

BILLY Sure.
(Getting nervously to his feet)

ROGER Sure. All right. We can be doin' it to the music.
(He plugs the radio into the floor outlet as BILLY *bolts for the door.)*

BILLY I gotta go pee.

ROGER You watch out for the snakes.

BILLY It's the snowmen, man; the snowmen.
*(*BILLY *is gone and "Ruby," sung by Ray Charles, comes from the radio. For a moment, as the music plays,* ROGER *watches* RICHIE *wander about the room, pouring little splashes of wax onto the floor. Then* RICHIE *moves to his bed and lies down, and* ROGER, *shaking his head, starts leisurely to spread the wax, with* RICHIE *watching.)*

RICHIE How come you and Billy take all this so seriously—you know.

ROGER What?

RICHIE This army nonsense. You're always shining your brass and keeping your footlocker neat and your locker so neat. There's no point to any of it.

ROGER We here, ain't we, Richie? We in the army.
(Still working the wax)

RICHIE There's no point to any of it. And doing those push-ups, the two of you.

ROGER We just see a lot a things the same way is all. Army ought to be a serious business, even if sometimes it ain't.

RICHIE You're lucky, you know, the two of you. Having each other for friends the way you do. I never had that kind of friend ever. Not even when I was little.

ROGER *(After a pause during which* ROGER, *working, sort of peeks at* RICHIE *every now and then)* You ain't really inta that stuff, are you, Richie?

(It is a question that is a statement.)

RICHIE *(Coyly he looks at* ROGER.*)* What stuff is that, Roger?

ROGER That fag stuff, man. You know. You ain't really into it, are you? You maybe messed in it a little is all—am I right?

RICHIE I'm very weak, Roger. And by that I simply mean that if I have an impulse to do something, I don't know how to deny myself. If I feel like doing something, I just do it. I . . . will . . . admit to sometimes wishin' I . . . was a little more like you . . . and Billy, even, but not to any severe extent.

ROGER But that's such a bad scene, Rich. You don't want that. Nobody wants that. Nobody wants to be a punk. Not nobody. You wanna know what I think it is? You just got in with the wrong bunch. Am I right? You just got in with a bad bunch. That can happen. And that's what I think happened to you. I bet you never had a chance to really run with the boys before. I mean, regular normal guys like Billy and me. How'd you come in the army, huh, Richie? You get drafted?

RICHIE No.

ROGER That's my point, see.

(He has stopped working. He stands, leaning on the mop, looking at RICHIE.*)*

RICHIE About four years ago, I went to this party. I was very young, and I went to this party with a friend who was older and . . . this "fag stuff," as you call it, was going on . . . so I did it.

ROGER And then you come in the army to get away from it, right? Huh?

RICHIE I don't know.

ROGER Sure.

RICHIE I don't know, Roger.

ROGER Sure; sure. And now you're gettin' a chance to run with the boys for a little, you'll get yourself straightened around. I know it for a fact; I know that thing.
(From off there is the sudden loud bellowing sound of Sergeant ROONEY.)

ROONEY THERE AIN'T BEEN NO SOLDIERS IN THIS CAMP BUT ME. I BEEN THE ONLY ONE—I BEEN THE ONLY ME!
(And BILLY *comes dashing into the room.)*

BILLY Oh, boy.

ROGER Guess who?

ROONEY FOR SO LONG I BEEN THE ONLY GODDAMN ONE!

BILLY *(Leaping onto his bed and covering his face with a* Playboy *magazine as* RICHIE *is trying to disappear under his sheets and blankets and* ROGER *is trying to get the wax put away so he can get into his own bunk)* Hut who hee whor— he's got some Yo-Yo with him, Rog!

ROGER Huh?
(As COKES *and* ROONEY *enter. Both are in fatigues and drunk and big-bellied. They are in their fifties, their hair whitish and cut short. Both men carry whiskey bottles, beer bottles.* COKES *is a little neater than* ROONEY, *his fatigue jacket tucked in and not so rumpled, and he wears canvas-sided jungle boots.* ROONEY, *very disheveled, chomps on the stub of a big cigar. They swagger in, looking for fun, and stand there side by side.)*

ROONEY What kinda platoon I got here? You buncha shit sacks. Everybody look sharp.
  (The three boys lie there, unmoving.)
Off and on!

COKES OFF AND ON!
  (He seems barely conscious, wavering as he stands.)

ROGER What's happenin', Sergeant?

ROONEY *(Shoving his bottle of whiskey at* ROGER, *who is sitting up)* Shut up, Moore! You want a belt?
  (Splashing whiskey on ROGER'S *chest)*

ROGER How can I say no?

COKES My name is Cokes!

BILLY *(Rising to sit on the side of his bed)* How about me, too?

COKES You wait your turn.

ROONEY *(He looks at the three of them as if they are fools. Indicates* COKES *with a gesture.)* Don't you see what I got here?

BILLY Who do I follow for my turn?

ROONEY *(Suddenly, crazily petulant)* Don't you see what I got here? Everybody on their feet and at attention!
  *(*BILLY *and* ROGER *climb from their bunks and stand at attention. They don't know what* ROONEY *is mad at.)*
I mean it!
  *(*RICHIE *bounds to the position of attention.)*
This here is my friend, who in addition just come back from the war! The goddamn war! He been to it and he come back.

(ROONEY *is patting* COKES *gently, proudly.)*
The man's a fuckin' hero!
(ROONEY *hugs* COKES, *almost kissing him on the cheek.)*
He's always been a fuckin' hero.
(COKES, *embarrassed in his stupor, kind of wobbles a little from side to side.)*

COKES No-o-o-o-o-o . . .
(*And* ROONEY *grabs him, starts pushing him toward* BILLY'S *footlocker.)*

ROONEY Show 'em your boots, Cokes. Show 'em your jungle boots.
(*With a long, clumsy step,* COKES *climbs onto the foot-locker,* ROONEY *supporting him from behind and then bending to lift one of* COKES' *booted feet and display it for the boys.)*
Lookee that boot. That ain't no everyday goddamn army boot. That is a goddamn jungle boot! That green canvas is a jungle boot 'cause a the heat, and them little holes in the bottom are so the water can run out when you been walkin' in a lotta water like in a jungle swamp.
(*He is extremely proud of all this; he looks at them.)*
The army ain't no goddamn fool. You see a man wearin' boots like that, you might as well see he's got a chestful a medals, 'cause he been to the war. He don't have no boots like that unless he been to the war! Which is where I'm goin' and all you slaphappy motherfuckers, too. Got to go kill some gooks.
(*He is nodding at them, smiling.)*
That's right.

COKES (*Bursting loudly from his stupor*) Gonna piss on 'em. Old booze. 'At's what I did. Piss in the rivers. Goddamn GI's secret weapon is old booze and he's pissin' it in all

their runnin' water. Makes 'em yellow. Ahhhha ha, ha, ha!
(He laughs and laughs, and ROONEY *laughs, too, hugging*
COKES.*)*

ROONEY Me and Cokesy been in so much shit together we
oughta be brown.
(And then he catches himself, looks at ROGER.*)*
Don't take no offense at that, Moore. We been swimmin'
in it. One Hundred and First Airborne, together. One-oh-
one. Screamin' goddamn Eagles!
*(Looking at each other, face to face, eyes glinting, they
make sudden loud screaming-eagle sounds.)*
This ain't the army; you punks ain't in the army. You ain't
ever seen the army. The army is Airborne! Airborne!

COKES *(Beginning to stomp his feet)* Airborne, Airborne! ALL
THE WAY!
(As RICHIE, *amused and hoping for a drink, too, reaches
out toward* ROONEY*)*

RICHIE Sergeant, Sergeant, I can have a little drink, too.
*(*ROONEY *looks at him and clutches the bottle.)*

ROONEY Are you kiddin' me? You gotta be kiddin' me.
(He looks to ROGER.*)*
He's kiddin' me, ain't he, Moore?
(And then to BILLY *and then to* COKES*)*
Ain't he, Cokesy?
*(*COKES *steps forward and down with a thump, taking
charge for his bewildered friend.)*

COKES Don't you know you are tryin' to take the booze from
the hand a the future goddamn Congressional Honor win-
ner . . . Medal . . . ?
(And he looks lovingly at ROONEY. *He beams.)*
Ole Rooney, Ole Rooney.
(He hugs ROONEY's *head.)*

He almost done it already.

(And ROONEY, overwhelmed, starts screaming "Agggggg-hhhhhhhhhh," a screaming-eagle sound, and making claw-ing eagle gestures at the air. He jumps up and down, stomping his feet. COKES instantly joins in, stomping and jumping and yelling.)

ROONEY Let's show these shit sacks how men are men jumpin' outa planes. Aggggggghhhhhhhhhh.

(Stomping and yelling, they move in a circle, ROONEY followed by COKES.)

A plane fulla yellin' stompin' men!

COKES All yellin' stompin' men!

(They yell and stomp, making eagle sounds, and then ROONEY leaps up on BILLY'S bed and runs the length of it until he is on the footlocker, COKES still on the floor, stomping. ROONEY makes a gesture of hooking his rip cord to the line inside the plane. They yell louder and louder and ROONEY leaps high into the air, yelling, "GERONIMO-o-o-o!" as COKES leaps onto the locker and then high into the air, bellowing, "GERONIMO-o-o-o!" They stand side by side, their arms held up in the air as if grasping the shroud lines of open chutes. They seem to float there in silence.)

What a feelin' . . .

ROONEY Beautiful feelin' . . .

(For a moment more they float there, adrift in the room, the sky, their memory. COKES smiles at ROONEY.)

COKES Remember that one guy, O'Flannigan . . . ?

ROONEY (Nodding, smiling, remembering) O'Flannigan . . .

COKES He was this one guy . . . O'Flannigan . . .

(He moves now toward the boys, BILLY, ROGER and RICHIE, who have gathered on ROGER'S bed and footlocker.

ROONEY *follows several steps, then drifts backward onto* BILLY's *bed, where he sits and then lies back, listening to* COKES.*)*
We was testing chutes where you could just pull a lever by your ribs here when you hit the ground—see—and the chute would come off you, because it was just after a whole bunch a guys had been dragged to death in an unexpected and terrible wind at Fort Bragg. So they wanted you to be able to release the chute when you hit if there was a bad wind when you hit. So O'Flannigan was this kinda joker who had the goddamn sense a humor of a clown and nerves, I tell you, of steel, and he says he's gonna release the lever midair, then reach up, grab the lines and float on down, hanging.
(His hand paws at the air, seeking a rope that isn't there.)
So I seen him pull the lever at five hundred feet and he reaches up to two fistfuls a air, the chute's twenty feet above him, and he went into the ground like a knife.
(The bottle, held high over his head, falls through the air to the bed, all watching it.)

BILLY Geezus.

ROONEY *(Nodding gently)* Didn't get to sing the song, I bet.

COKES *(Standing, staring at the fallen bottle)* No way.

RICHIE What song?

ROONEY *(He rises up, mysteriously angry.)* Shit sack! Shit sack!

RICHIE What song, Sergeant Rooney?

ROONEY "Beautiful Streamer," shit sack.
*(*COKES, *gone into another reverie, is staring skyward.)*

COKES I saw this one guy—never forget it. Never.

BILLY That's Richie, Sergeant Rooney. He's a beautiful screamer.

RICHIE He said "streamer," not "screamer," asshole.

(**COKES** *is still in his reverie.*)

COKES This guy with his chute goin' straight up above him in a streamer, like a tulip, only white, you know. All twisted and never gonna open. Like a big icicle sticking straight up above him. He went right by me. We met eyes, sort of. He was lookin' real puzzled. He looks right at me. Then he looks up in the air at the chute, then down at the ground.

ROONEY Did *he* sing it?

COKES He didn't sing it. He started going like this.

(**COKES** *reaches desperately upward with both hands and begins to claw at the sky while his legs pump up and down.*)

Like he was gonna climb right up the air.

RICHIE Ohhhhh, Geezus.

BILLY God.

(**ROONEY** *has collapsed backward on* **BILLY'S** *bed and he lies there and then he rises.*)

ROONEY Cokes got the Silver Star for rollin' a barrel a oil down a hill in Korea into forty-seven chinky Chinese gooks who were climbin' up the hill and when he shot into it with his machine gun, it blew them all to grape jelly.

(**COKES,** *rocking a little on his feet, begins to hum and then sing "Beautiful Streamer," to the tune of Stephen Foster's "Beautiful Dreamer."*)

COKES "Beautiful streamer, open for me ... The sky is above me ..."

(*And then the singing stops.*)

But the one I remember is this little guy in his spider hole, which is a hole in the ground with a lid over it.

(*And he is using* **RICHIE'S** *footlocker before him as the spider hole. He has fixed on it, is moving toward it.*)

And he shot me in the ass as I was runnin' by, but the bullet hit me so hard—

(His body kind of jerks and he runs several steps.)

—it knocked me into this ditch where he couldn't see me. I got behind him.

(Now at the head of RICHIE's *bed, he begins to creep along the side of the bed as if sneaking up on the footlocker.)*

Crawlin'. And I dropped a grenade into his hole.

(He jams a whiskey bottle into the footlocker, then slams down the lid.)

Then sat on the lid, him bouncin' and yellin' under me. Bouncin' and yellin' under the lid. I could hear him. Feel him. I just sat there.

(Silence. ROONEY *waits, thinking, then leans forward.)*

ROONEY He was probably singin' it.

COKES *(Sitting there)* I think so.

ROONEY You think we should let 'em hear it?

BILLY We're good boys. We're good ole boys.

COKES *(Jerking himself to his feet, he staggers sideways to join* ROONEY *on* BILLY's *bed.)* I don't care who hears it, I just wanna be singin' it.

*(*ROONEY *rises; he goes to the boys on* ROGER's *bed and speaks to them carefully, as if lecturing people on something of great importance.)*

ROONEY You listen up; you just be listenin' up, 'cause if you hear it right you can maybe stop bein' shit sacks. This is what a man sings, he's goin' down through the air, his chute don't open.

(Flopping back down on the bunk beside COKES, ROONEY *looks at* COKES *and then at the boys. The two older men put their arms around each other and they begin to sing.)*

ROONEY AND COKES *(Singing)*
> Beautiful streamer,
> Open for me,
> The sky is above me,
> But no canopy.

BILLY *(Murmuring)* I don't believe it.

ROONEY AND COKES
> Counted ten thousand,
> Pulled on the cord.
> My chute didn't open,
> I shouted, "Dear Lord."
>
> Beautiful streamer,
> This looks like the end,
> The earth is below me,
> My body won't bend.
>
> Just like a mother
> Watching o'er me,
> Beautiful streamer,
> Ohhhhh, open for me.

ROGER Un-fuckin'-believable.

ROONEY *(Beaming with pride)* Ain't that a beauty.
(And then COKES *topples forward onto his face and flops limply to his side. The three boys leap to their feet.* ROONEY *lunges toward* COKES.*)*

RICHIE Sergeant!

ROONEY Cokie! Cokie!

BILLY Jesus.

ROGER Hey!

COKES Huh? Huh?

(*COKES sits up. ROONEY is kneeling beside him.*)

ROONEY Jesus, Cokie.

COKES I been doin' that; I been doin' that. It don't mean nothin'.

ROONEY No, no.

COKES (*Pushing at ROONEY, who is trying to help him get back to the bed. ROONEY agrees with everything COKES is now saying and the noises he makes are little animal noises.*) I told 'em when they wanted to send me back I ain't got no leukemia; they wanna check it. They think I got it. I don't think I got it. Rooney? Whata you think?

ROONEY No.

COKES My mother had it. She had it. Just 'cause she did and I been fallin' down.

ROONEY It don't mean nothin'.

COKES (*He lunges back and up onto the bed.*) I tole 'em I fall down 'cause I'm drunk. I'm drunk all the time.

ROONEY You'll be goin' back over there with me, is what I know, Cokie.
(*He is patting COKES, nodding, dusting him off.*)
That's what I know.
(*As BILLY comes up to them, almost seeming to want to be a part of the intimacy they are sharing*)

BILLY That was somethin', Sergeant Cokes. Jesus.
(*ROONEY whirls on him, ferocious, pushing him.*)

ROONEY Get the fuck away, Wilson! Whata you know? Get the fuck away. You don't know shit. Get away! You don't know shit.

(And he turns to COKES, *who is standing up from the bed.)*
Me and Cokes are goin' to the war zone like we oughta.
Gonna blow it to shit.
(He is grabbing at COKES, *who is laughing. They are both
laughing.* ROONEY *whirls on the boys.)*
Ohhh, I'm gonna be so happy to be away from you assholes;
you pussies. Not one regular army people among you possible. I swear it to my mother who is holy. You just be
watchin' the papers for doin' darin' brave deeds. 'Cause
we're old hands at it. Makin' shit disappear. Goddamn
whooosh!

COKES Whooosh!

ROONEY Demnalitions. Me and . . .
(And then he knows he hasn't said it right.)
Me and Cokie . . . Demnal . . . Demnali . . .

RICHIE *(Still sitting on* ROGER'S *bed)* You can do it, Sergeant.

BILLY Get it.
(He stands by the lockers and ROONEY *glares at him.)*

ROGER 'Cause you're cool with dynamite, is what you're tryin'
to say.

ROONEY *(Charging at* ROGER, *bellowing)* Shut the fuck up,
that's what you can do; and go to goddamn sleep. You
buncha shit . . . sacks. Buncha mothers—know-it-all moth-
erin' shit sacks—that's what you are.

COKES *(Shoulders back, he is taking charge.)* Just goin' to sleep
is what you can do, 'cause Rooney and me fought it through
two wars already and we can make it through this one
more and leukemia that comes or doesn't come—who gives
a shit? Not guys like us. We're goin' just pretty as pie. And
it's lights-out time, ain't it, Rooney?

ROONEY Past it. goddammit. So the lights are goin' out.
>(*There is fear in the room, and the three boys rush to their wall lockers, where they start to strip to their underwear, preparing for bed. ROONEY paces the room, watching them, glaring.*)

Somebody's gotta teach you soldierin'. You hear me? Or you wanna go outside and march around awhile, huh? We can do that if you wanna. Huh? You tell me? Marchin' or sleepin'? What's it gonna be?

RICHIE (*Rushing to get into bed*) Flick out the ole lights, Sergeant; that's what we say.

BILLY (*Climbing into bed*) Put out the ole lights.

ROGER (*In bed and pulling up the covers*) Do it.

COKES Shut up.
>(*He rocks forward and back, trying to stand at attention. He is saying good night.*)

And that's an order. Just shut up. I got grenades down the hall. I got a pistol. I know where to get nitro. You don't shut up, I'll blow . . . you . . . to . . . fuck.
>(*Making a military left face. he stalks to the wall switch and turns the lights out. ROONEY is watching proudly, as COKES faces the boys again. He looks at them.*)

That's right.
>(*In the dark, there is only a spill of light from the hall coming in the open door. COKES and ROONEY put their arms around each other and go out the door, leaving it partly open. RICHIE, ROGER and BILLY lie in their bunks, staring. They do not move. They lie there. The sergeants seem to have vanished soundlessly once they went out the door. Light touches each of the boys as they lie there.*)

ROGER (*He does not move.*) Lord have mercy, if that ain't a pair. If that ain't one pair a beauties.

BILLY Oh, yeh.
(He does not move.)

ROGER Too much, man—too, too much.

RICHIE They made me sad; but I loved them, sort of. Better than movies.

ROGER Too much. Too, too much.
(Silence)

BILLY What time is it?

ROGER Sleep time, men. Sleep time.
(Silence)

BILLY Right.

ROGER They were somethin'. Too much.

BILLY Too much.

RICHIE Night.

ROGER Night.
(Silence)
Night, Billy.

BILLY Night.
*(**RICHIE** stirs in his bed. **ROGER** turns onto his side. **BILLY** is motionless.)*

BILLY I . . . had a buddy, Rog—and this is the whole thing, this is the whole point—a kid I grew up with, played ball with in high school, and he was a tough little cat, a real bad man sometimes. Used to have gangster pictures up in his room. Anyway, we got into this deal where we'd drive on down to the big city, man, you know, hit the bad spots, let some queer pick us up . . . sort of . . . long enough to buy us some good stuff. It was kinda the thing to do for a while, and we all did it, the whole gang of us. So we'd let these cats pick us up, most of 'em old guys, and they were hurtin' and happy as hell to have us, and we'd get a lot of free booze, maybe a meal, and we'd turn 'em on. Then pretty soon they'd ask us did we want to go over to their place. Sure, we'd say, and order one more drink, and then when we hit the street, we'd tell 'em to kiss off. We'd call 'em fag and queer and jazz like that and tell 'em to kiss off. And Frankie, the kid I'm tellin' you about, he had a mean streak in him and if they gave us a bad time at all, he'd put 'em down. That's the way he was. So that kinda jazz went on and on for sort of a long time and it was a good deal if we were low on cash or needed a laugh and it went on for a while. And then Frankie—one day he come up to me—and he says he was goin' home with the guy he was with. He said, what the hell, what did it matter? And he's sayin'— Frankie's sayin'—why don't I tag along? What the hell, he's sayin', what does it matter who does it to you, some broad or some old guy, you close your eyes, a mouth's a mouth, it don't matter—that's what he's sayin'. I tried to talk him out of it, but he wasn't hearin' anything I was sayin'. So the next day, see, he calls me up to tell me about it. Okay, okay, he says, it was a cool scene, he says; they played poker, a buck minimum, and he made a fortune. Frankie was eatin' it up, man. It was a pretty way to live, he says. So he stayed at it, and he had this nice little girl he was goin' with at the time. You know the way a real bad cat can sometimes do that—have a good little girl who's crazy about him and he is for her, too, and he's a different cat when he's with her?

ROGER Uh-huh.

(The hall light slants across **BILLY'S** *face.)*

BILLY Well, that was him and Linda, and then one day he dropped her, he cut her loose. He was hooked, man. He was

into it, with no way he knew out—you understand what
I'm sayin'? He had got his ass hooked. He had never
thought he would and then one day he woke up and he
was on it. He just hadn't been told, that's the way I figure
it; somebody didn't tell him somethin' he shoulda been
told and he come to me wailin' one day, man, all broke up
and wailin', my boy Frankie, my main man, and he was a
fag. He was a faggot, black Roger, and I'm not lyin'. I am
not lyin' to you.

ROGER Damn.

BILLY So that's the whole thing, man; that's the whole thing.
(*Silence. They lie there.*)

ROGER Holy ... Christ. Richie ... you hear him? You hear
what he said?

RICHIE He's a storyteller.

ROGER What you mean?

RICHIE I mean, he's a storyteller, all right; he tells stories, all
right.

ROGER What are we into now? You wanna end up like that
friend a his, or you don't believe what he said? Which are
you sayin'?
(*The door bursts open. The sounds of machine guns and
cannon are being made by someone, and* CARLYLE, *drunk
and playing, comes crawling in.* ROGER, RICHIE *and* BILLY
all pop up, startled, to look at him.)
Hey, hey, what's happenin'?

BILLY Who's happenin'?

ROGER You attackin' or you retreatin', man?

CARLYLE *(Looking up; big grin)* Hey, baby . . . ?
(Continues shooting, crawling. The three boys look at each other.)

ROGER What's happenin', man? Whatcha doin'?

CARLYLE I dunno, soul; I dunno. Practicin' my duties, my new abilities.
(Half sitting, he flops onto his side, starts to crawl.)
The low crawl, man; like I was taught in basic, that's what I'm doin'. You gotta know your shit, man, else you get your ass blown so far away you don't ever see it again. Oh, sure, you guys don't care. I know it. You got it made. You got it made. I don't got it made. You got a little home here, got friends, people to talk to. I got nothin'. You got jobs they probably ain't ever gonna ship you out, you got so important jobs. I got no job. They don't even wanna give me a job. I know it. They are gonna kill me. They are gonna send me over there to get me killed, goddammit. WHAT'S A MATTER WITH ALL YOU PEOPLE?
(The anger explodes out of the grieving and ROGER rushes to kneel beside CARLYLE. He speaks gently, firmly.)
Hey, man, get cool, get some cool; purchase some cool, man.

CARLYLE Awwwww . . .
(Clumsily, he turns away.)

ROGER Just hang in there.

CARLYLE I don't wanna be no DEAD man. I don't wanna be the one they all thinkin' is so stupid he's the only one'll go, they tell him; they don't even have to give him a job. I got thoughts, man, in my head; alla time, burnin', burnin' thoughts a understandin'.

ROGER Don't you think we know that, man? It ain't the way you're sayin' it.

ROONEY AND COKES (Kenneth McMillan and Dolph Sweet):
Beautiful streamer,
Open for me,
The sky is above me,
But no canopy.
BILLY (Paul Rudd): I don't believe it.

ROGER (Terry Alexander): Now let us do fifteen or twenty p-shups and get over to that gymnasium, like I been sayin'. Then we can take our civvies with us—we can shower and change at the gym.
BILLY (Paul Rudd): I don't know; I don't know . . . what it is I'm feelin'. Sick like.

CARLYLE (Dorian Harewood): HEY RICHIE! I just got this question I asked, I got no answer.
RICHIE (Peter Evans): I don't know . . . what . . . you mean.
CARLYLE: I heard me. I understood me. "How long you been a punk?" is the question
I asked—have you got a reply?

CARLYLE (Dorian Harewood): That you blood. The blood inside you, you don't ever see
it there—take a look how easy it come out. . . .

RICHIE (Peter Evans): Carlyle, don't hurt anybody more!

LIEUTENANT (Arlen Dean Snyder): You shut the hell up, soldier. I am ordering you.

CARLYLE (Dorian Harewood): I don't understand you people! Don't you understand when a man be talkin' English at you to say his mind? I have quit the army!

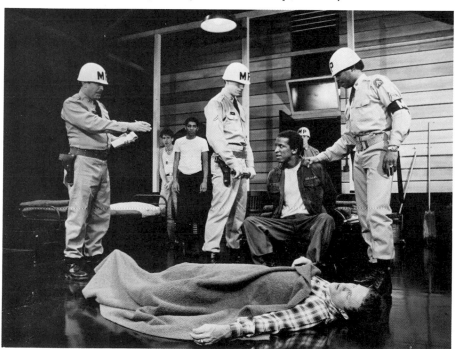

COKES (Dolph Sweet):
    Yo no som lo no,
    Ung toe lo knee . . .

CARLYLE It is.

ROGER No. I mean, we all probably gonna go. We all probably gonna have to go.

CARLYLE No-o-o-o-o.

ROGER I mean it.

CARLYLE *(Suddenly he nearly topples over.)* I am very drunk. *(And he looks up at* ROGER.*)* You think so?

ROGER I'm sayin' so. And I am sayin', "No sweat." No point. *(*CARLYLE *angrily pushes at* ROGER, *knocking him backward.)*

CARLYLE Awwwww, dammit, dammit, mother . . . shit . . . it . . . ohhhhhhh.
(Sliding to the floor, the rage and anguish softening into only breathing)
I mean it. I mean it.
(Silence. He lies there.)

ROGER What . . . a you doin' . . . ?

CARLYLE Huh?

ROGER I don't know what you're up to on our freshly mopped floor.

CARLYLE Gonna go sleep—okay? No sweat . . .
(Suddenly very polite, he is looking up.)
Can I, soul? Izzit all right?

ROGER Sure, man, sure, if you wanna, but why don't you go where you got a bed? Don't you like beds?

CARLYLE Dunno where's zat. My bed. I can' fin' it. I can' fin'

my own bed. I looked all over, but I can' fin' it anywhere.
GONE!
*(Slipping back down now, he squirms to make a nest. He
hugs his bottle.)*

ROGER *(Moving to his bunk, where he grabs a blanket)* Okay,
okay, man. But get on top a this, man.
*(He is spreading the blanket on the floor, trying to help
CARLYLE get on it.)*
Make it softer. C'mon, c'mon . . . get on this.
*(BILLY has risen with his own blanket, and is moving now
to hand it to ROGER.)*

BILLY Cat's hurtin', Rog.

ROGER Ohhhhh, yeh.

CARLYLE Ohhhhh . . . it was so sweet at home . . . it was so
sweet, baby; so-o-o good. They doin' dances make you wanna
cry. . . .
(Hugging the blankets now, he drifts in a kind of dream.)

ROGER I know, man.

CARLYLE So sweet . . . !
*(BILLY is moving back to his own bed, where, quietly, he
sits.)*

ROGER I know, man.

CARLYLE So sweet . . . !

ROGER Yeh.

CARLYLE How come I gotta be here?
*(On his way to the door to close it, ROGER falters, looks
at CARLYLE then moves on toward the door.)*

ROGER I dunno, Jim.
*(BILLY is sitting and watching, as ROGER goes on to the
door, gently closes it and returns to his bed.)*

BILLY I know why he's gotta be here, Roger. You wanna know? Why don't you ask me?

ROGER Okay. How come he gotta be here?

BILLY *(Smiling)* Freedom's frontier, man. That's why.

ROGER *(Settled on the edge of his bed and about to lie back)* Oh . . . yeh . . .
(As a distant bugle begins to play taps and RICHIE, *carrying a blanket, is approaching* CARLYLE. ROGER *settles back;* BILLY *is staring at* RICHIE; CARLYLE *does not stir; the bugle plays.)*
Bet that ole sarge don't live a year, Billy. Fuckin' blow his own ass sky high.
*(*RICHIE *has covered* CARLYLE. *He pats* CARLYLE'S *arm, and then straightens in order to return to his bed.)*

BILLY Richie . . . !
*(*BILLY'S *hissing voice freezes* RICHIE. *He stands, and then he starts again to move, and* BILLY'S *voice comes again and* RICHIE *cannot move.)*
Richie . . . how come you gotta keep doin' that stuff?
*(*ROGER *looks at* BILLY, *staring at* RICHIE, *who stands still as a stone over the sleeping* CARLYLE.)*
How come?

ROGER He dunno, man. Do you? You dunno, do you, Rich?

RICHIE No.

CARLYLE *(From deep in his sleep and grieving)* It . . . was . . . so . . . pretty . . . !

RICHIE No.
(The lights are fading with the last soft notes of taps.)

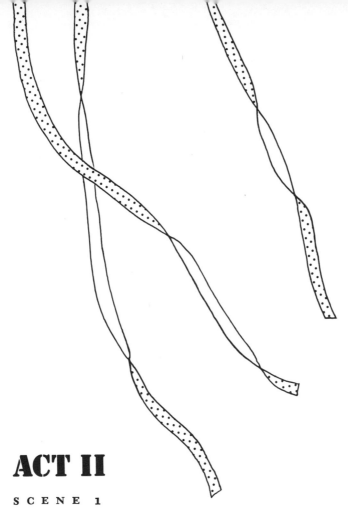

ACT II

S C E N E 1

Lights come up on the cadre room. It is late afternoon and BILLY is lying on his stomach, his head at the foot of the bed, his chin resting on his hands. He wears gym shorts and sweat socks; his T-shirt lies on the bed and his sneakers are on the floor. ROGER is at his footlocker, taking out a pair of sweat socks. His sneakers and his basketball are on his bed. He is wearing his khakis.

A silence passes, and then ROGER closes his footlocker and sits on his bed, where he starts lacing his sneakers, holding them on his lap.

BILLY Rog . . . you think I'm a busybody? In any way?
(*Silence.* ROGER *laces his sneakers.*)
Roger?

ROGER Huh? Uh-uh.

BILLY Some people do. I mean, back home.
(*He rolls slightly to look at* ROGER.)
Or that I didn't know how to behave. Sort of.

ROGER It's time we maybe get changed, don't you think?
(ROGER *rises and goes to his locker. He takes off his trousers, shoes and socks.*)

BILLY Yeh. I guess. I don't feel like it, though. I don't feel good, don't know why.

ROGER Be good for you, man; be good for you.
(*Pulling on his gym shorts,* ROGER *returns to his bed, carrying his shoes and socks.*)

BILLY Yeh.
(BILLY *sits up on the edge of his bed.* ROGER, *sitting, is bowed over, putting on his socks.*)
I mean, a lot a people thought like I didn't know how to behave in a simple way. You know? That I overcomplicated everything. I didn't think so. Don't think so. I just thought I was seein' complications that were there but nobody else saw.
(*He is struggling now to put on his T-shirt. He seems weary, almost weak.*)
I mean, Wisconsin's a funny place. All those clear-eyed people sayin' "Hello" and lookin' you straight in the eye. Everybody's good, you think, and happy and honest. And then there's all of a sudden a neighbor who goes mad as a hatter. I had a neighbor who came out of his house one morning with axes in both hands. He started then attackin' the cars that were driving up and down in front of his house. An'

we all knew why he did it, sorta.

(He pauses; he thinks.)

It made me wanna be a priest. I wanted to be a priest then. I was sixteen. Priests could help people. Could take away what hurt 'em. I wanted that, I thought. Somethin', huh?

ROGER *(He has the basketball in his hands.)* Yeh. But everybody's got feelin's like that sometimes.

BILLY I don't know.

ROGER You know, you oughta work on a little jump shot, my man. Get you some kinda fall-away jumper to go with that beauty of a hook. Make you tough out there.

BILLY Can't fuckin' do it. Not my game. I mean, like that bar we go to. You think I could get a job there bartendin', maybe? I could learn the ropes.

(He is watching ROGER, *who has risen to walk to his locker.)*

You think I could get a job there off-duty hours?

ROGER *(Pulling his locker open to display the pinup on the inside of the door)* You don't want no job. It's that little black-haired waitress you wantin' to know.

BILLY No, man. Not really.

ROGER It's okay. She tough, man.

(He begins to remove his uniform shirt. He will put on an O.D. T-shirt to go to the gym.)

BILLY I mean, not the way you're sayin' it, is all. Sure, there's somethin' about her. I don't know what. I ain't even spoke to her yet. But somethin'. I mean, what's she doin' there? When she's dancin', it's like she knows somethin'. She's degradin' herself, I sometimes feel. You think she is?

ROGER Man, you don't even know the girl. She's workin'.

BILLY I'd like to talk to her. Tell her stuff. Find out about her. Sometimes I'm thinkin' about her and it and I got a job there, I get to know her and she and I get to be real tight, man—close, you know. Maybe we screw, maybe we don't. It's nice . . . whatever.

ROGER Sure. She a real fine-lookin' chippy, Billy. Got nice cakes. Nice little titties.

BILLY I think she's smart, too.
  (ROGER *starts laughing so hard he almost falls into his locker.*)
Oh, all I do is talk. "Yabba-yabba." I mean, my mom and dad are really terrific people. How'd they ever end up with somebody so weird as me?
  (ROGER *moves to him, jostles him.*)

ROGER I'm tellin' you, the gym and a little ball is what you need. Little exercise. Little bumpin' into people. The soul is tellin' you.
  (BILLY *rises and goes to his locker, where he starts putting on his sweat clothes.*)

BILLY I mean, Roger, you remember how we met in P Company? Both of us brand-new. You started talkin' to me. You just started talkin' to me and you didn't stop.

ROGER (*Hardly looking up*) Yeh.

BILLY Did you see somethin' in me made you pick me?

ROGER I was talkin' to everybody, man. For that whole day. Two whole days. You was just the first one to talk back friendly. Though you didn't say much, as I recall.

BILLY The first white person, you mean.
  (*Wearing his sweat pants,* BILLY *is now at his bed, putting on his sneakers.*)

ROGER Yeh. I was tryin' to come outa myself a little. Do like the fuckin' head shrinker been tellin' me to stop them fuckin' headaches I was havin', you know. Now let us do fifteen or twenty push-ups and get over to that gymnasium, like I been sayin'. Then we can take our civvies with us— we can shower and change at the gym.

(ROGER *crosses to* BILLY, *who flops down on his belly on the bed.*)

BILLY I don't know . . . I don't know what it is I'm feelin'. Sick like.

(ROGER *forces* BILLY *up onto his feet and shoves him playfully downstage, where they both fall forward into the push-up position, side by side.*)

ROGER Do 'em, trooper. Do 'em. Get it.

(ROGER *starts.* BILLY *joins in. After five,* ROGER *realizes that* BILLY *has his knees on the floor. They start again. This time,* BILLY *counts in double time. They start again. At about "seven,"* RICHIE *enters. Neither* BILLY *nor* ROGER *sees him. They keep going.*)

ROGER AND BILLY . . . seven, eight, nine, ten . . .

RICHIE No, no; no, no; no, no, no. That's not it; that's not it. (*They keep going, yelling the numbers louder and louder.*)

ROGER AND BILLY . . . eleven, twelve, thirteen . . .

(RICHIE *crosses to his locker and gets his bottle of cologne, and then returning to the center of the room to stare at them, he stands there dabbing cologne on his face.*)

ROGER AND BILLY . . . fourteen, fifteen.

RICHIE You'll never get it like that. You're so far apart and you're both humping at the same time. And all that counting. It's so unromantic.

ROGER (*Rising and moving to his bed to pick up the basketball*) We was exercisin', Richard. You heard a that?

RICHIE Call it what you will, Roger.
> *(With a flick of his wrist, ROGER tosses the basketball to BILLY.)*

Everybody has their own cute little pet names for it.

BILLY Hey!
> *(And he tosses the ball at RICHIE, hitting him in the chest, sending the cologne bottle flying. RICHIE yelps, as BILLY retrieves the ball and, grabbing up his sweat jacket from the bed, heads for the door. ROGER, at his own locker, has taken out his suit bag of civilian clothes.)*

You missed.

RICHIE Billy, Billy, Billy, please, please, the ruffian approach will not work with me. It impresses me not even one tiny little bit. All you've done is spill my cologne.
> *(He bends to pick up the cologne from the floor.)*

BILLY That was my aim.

ROGER See you.
> *(BILLY is passing RICHIE. Suddenly RICHIE sprays BILLY with cologne, some of it getting on ROGER, as ROGER and BILLY, groaning and cursing at RICHIE, rush out the door.)*

RICHIE Try the more delicate approach next time, Bill.
> *(Having crossed to the door, he stands a moment, leaning against the frame. Then he bounces to BILLY's bed, sings "He's just my Bill," and squirts cologne on the pillow. At his locker, he deposits the cologne, takes off his shirt, shoes and socks. Removing a hard-cover copy of Pauline Kael's* I Lost It at the Movies *from the top shelf of the locker, he bounds to the center of the room and tosses the book the rest of the way to the bed. Quite pleased with himself, he fidgets, pats his stomach, then lowers himself into the push-up position, goes to his knees and stands up.)*

Am I out of my fucking mind? Those two are crazy. I'm not crazy.

(RICHIE *pivots and strides to his locker. With an ashtray, a pack of matches and a pack of cigarettes, he hurries to his bed and makes himself comfortable to read, his head propped up on a pillow. Settling himself, he opens the book, finds his place, thinks a little, starts to read. For a moment he lies there. And then* CARLYLE *steps into the room. He comes through the doorway looking to his left and right. He comes several steps into the room and looks at* RICHIE. RICHIE *sees him. They look at each other.*)

CARLYLE Ain't nobody here, man?

RICHIE Hello, Carlyle. How are you today?

CARLYLE Ain't nobody here?
(*He is nervous and angrily disappointed.*)

RICHIE Who do you want?

CARLYLE Where's the black boy?

RICHIE Roger? My God, why do you keep calling him that? Don't you know his name yet? Roger. Roger.
(*He thickens his voice at this, imitating someone very stupid.* CARLYLE *stares at him.*)

CARLYLE Yeh. Where is he?

RICHIE I am not his keeper, you know. I am not his private secretary, you know.

CARLYLE I do not know. I do not know. That is why I am asking. I come to see him. You are here. I ask you. I don't know. I mean, Carlyle made a fool outa himself comin' in here the other night, talkin' on and on like how he did. Lay on the floor. He remember. You remember? It all one hype, man; that all one hype. You know what I mean. That ain't the real Carlyle was in here. This one here and now the real Carlyle. Who the real Richie?

RICHIE Well . . . the real Richie . . . has gone home. To Manhattan. I, however, am about to read this book.
(Which he again starts to try to do)

CARLYLE Oh. Shit. Jus' you the only one here, then, huh?

RICHIE So it would seem.
(He looks at the air and then under the bed as if to find someone.)
So it would seem. Did you hear about Martin?

CARLYLE What happened to Martin? I ain't seen him.

RICHIE They are shipping him home. Someone told about what he did to himself. I don't know who.

CARLYLE Wasn't me. Not me. I keep that secret.

RICHIE I'm sure you did.
(Rising, walking toward CARLYLE and the door, cigarette pack in hand)
You want a cigarette? Or don't you smoke? Or do you have to go right away?
(Closing the door)
There's a chill sometimes coming down the hall, I don't know from where.
(Crossing back to his bed and climbing in)
And I think I've got the start of a little cold. Did you want the cigarette?
(CARLYLE is staring at him. Then he examines the door and looks again at RICHIE. He stares at RICHIE, thinking, and then he walks toward him.)

CARLYLE You know what I bet? I been lookin' at you real close. It just a way I got about me. And I bet if I was to hang my boy out in front of you, my big boy, man, you'd start wantin' to touch him. Be beggin' and talkin' sweet to ole Carlyle. Am I right or wrong?
(He leans over RICHIE.*)*
What do you say?

RICHIE Pardon?

CARLYLE You heard me. Ohhh. I am so restless, I don't even understand it. My big black boy is what I was talkin' about. My thing, man; my rope, Jim. HEY, RICHIE!
(And he lunges, then moves his fingers through RICHIE'S *hair.)*
How long you been a punk? Can you hear me? Am I clear? Do I talk funny?
(He is leaning close.)
Can you smell the gin on my mouth?

RICHIE I mean, if you really came looking for Roger, he and Billy are gone to the gymnasium. They were—

CARLYLE No.
(He slides down on the bed, his arm placed over RICHIE'S *legs.)*
I got no athletic abilities. I got none. No moves. I don't know. HEY, RICHIE!
(Leaning close again)
I just got this question I asked. I got no answer.

RICHIE I don't know . . . what . . . you mean.

CARLYLE I heard me. I understood me. "How long you been a punk?" is the question I asked. Have you got a reply?

RICHIE *(Confused, irritated, but fascinated)* Not to that question.

CARLYLE Who do if you don't? I don't. How'm I gonna?
(*Suddenly there is whistling in the hall, as if someone
might enter, footsteps approaching, and* RICHIE *leaps to
his feet and scurries away toward the door, tucking in his
undershirt as he goes.*)
Man, don't you wanna talk to me? Don't you wanna talk
to ole Carlyle?

RICHIE Not at the moment.

CARLYLE (*He is rising, starting after* RICHIE, *who stands nervously near* ROGER'S *bed.*) I want to talk to you, man; why
don't you want to talk to me? We can be friends. Talkin'
back and forth, sharin' thoughts and bein' happy.

RICHIE I don't think that's what you want.

CARLYLE (*He is very near to* RICHIE.) What do I want?

RICHIE I mean, to talk to me.
(RICHIE, *as if repulsed, crosses away. But it is hard to tell
if the move is genuine or coy.*)

CARLYLE What am I doin'? I am talkin'. DON'T YOU TELL ME
I AIN'T TALKIN' WHEN I AM TALKIN'! COURSE I AM. Bendin'
over backwards.
(*And pressing his hands against himself in his anger, he
has touched the grease on his shirt, the filth of his cloth-
ing, and this ignites the anger.*)
Do you know they still got me in that goddamn P Com-
pany? That goddamn transient company. It like they think
I ain't got no notion what a home is. No nose for no home
—like I ain't never had no home. I had a home. IT LIKE
THEY THINK THERE AIN'T NO PLACE FOR ME IN THIS MOTHER
ARMY BUT K.P. ALL SUDSY AND WRINKLED AND SWEATIN'.
EVERY DAY SINCE I GOT TO THIS SHIT HOUSE, MISTER! HOW

MANY TIMES YOU BEEN ON K.P.? WHEN'S THE LAST TIME YOU PULLED K.P.?

(He has roared down to where RICHIE *had moved, the rage possessing him.)*

RICHIE I'm E.D.

CARLYLE You E.D.? You E.D.? You Edie, are you? I didn't ask you what you friends call you, I asked you when's the last time you had K.P.?

RICHIE *(Edging toward his bed. He will go there, get and light a cigarette.)* E.D. is "Exempt from Duty."

CARLYLE *(Moving after* RICHIE*)* You ain't got no duties? What shit you talkin' about? Everybody in this fuckin' army got duties. That what the fuckin' army all about. You ain't got no duties, who got 'em?

RICHIE Because of my job, Carlyle. I have a very special job. And my friends don't call me Edie.
(Big smile)
They call me Irene.

CARLYLE That mean what you sayin' is you kiss ass for somebody, don't it? Good for you.
(Seemingly relaxed and gentle, he settles down on RICHIE'S *bed. He seems playful and charming.)*
You know the other night I was sleepin' there. You know.

RICHIE Yes.

CARLYLE *(Gleefully, enormously pleased)* You remember that? How come you remember that? You sweet.

RICHIE We don't have people sleeping on our floor that often, Carlyle.

CARLYLE But the way you crawl over in the night, gimme a big kiss on my joint. That nice.

RICHIE *(Shocked, he blinks.)* What?

CARLYLE Or did I dream that?

RICHIE *(Laughing in spite of himself)* My God, you're out-rageous!

CARLYLE Maybe you dreamed it.

RICHIE What . . . ? No. I don't know.

CARLYLE Maybe you did it, then; you didn't dream it.

RICHIE How come you talk so much?

CARLYLE I don't talk, man, who's gonna talk? YOU?
(He is laughing and amused, but there is an anger near the surface now, an ugliness.)
That bore me to death. I don't like nobody's voice but my own. I am so pretty. Don't like nobody else face.
(And then viciously, he spits out at RICHIE.)
You goddamn face ugly fuckin' queer punk!
(And RICHIE jumps in confusion.)

RICHIE What's the matter with you?

CARLYLE You goddamn ugly punk face. YOU UGLY!

RICHIE Nice mouth.

CARLYLE That's right. That's right. And you got a weird mouth. Like to suck joints.
(As RICHIE storms to his locker, throwing the book inside. He pivots, grabbing a towel, marching toward the door.)
Hey, you gonna jus' walk out on me? Where you goin'? You c'mon back. Hear?

RICHIE That's my bed, for chrissake.
(He lunges into the hall.)

CARLYLE You'd best.

(*Lying there, he makes himself comfortable. He takes a pint bottle from his back pocket.*)

You come back, Richie, I tell you a good joke. Make you laugh, make you cry.

(*He takes a big drink.*)

That's right. Ole Frank and Jesse, they got the stagecoach stopped, all the peoples lined up—Frank say, "All right, peoples, we gonna rape all the men and rob all the women." Jesse say, "Frank, no, no—that ain't it—we gonna—" And this one little man yell real loud, "You shut up, Jesse; Frank knows what he's doin'."

(*Loudly, he laughs and laughs.* BILLY *enters. Startled at the sight of* CARLYLE *there in* RICHIE's *bed,* BILLY *falters, as* CARLYLE *gestures toward him.*)

Hey, man . . . ! Hey, you know, they send me over to that Vietnam, I be cool, 'cause I been dodgin' bullets and shit since I been old enough to get on pussy make it happy to know me. I can get on, I can do my job.

(BILLY *looks weary and depressed. Languidly he crosses to his bed. He still wears his sweat clothes.* CARLYLE *studies him, then stares at the ceiling.*)

Yeh. I was just layin' here thinkin' that and you come in and out it come, words to say my feelin'. That my problem. That the black man's problem altogether. You ever considered that? Too much feelin'. He too close to everthing. He is, man; too close to his blood, to his body. It ain't that he don't have no good mind, but he BELIEVE in his body. Is . . . that Richie the only punk in this room, or is there more?

BILLY What?

CARLYLE The punk; is he the only punk?

(*Carefully he takes one of* RICHIE's *cigarettes and lights it.*)

BILLY He's all right.

CARLYLE I ain't askin' about the quality of his talent, but is he the only one, is my question?

BILLY *(He does not want to deal with this. He sits there.)* You get your orders yet?

CARLYLE Orders for what?

BILLY To tell you where you work.

CARLYLE I'm P Company, man. I work in P Company. I do K.P. That all. Don't deserve no more. Do you know I been in this army three months and ten days and everbody still doin' the same shit and sayin' the same shit and wearin' the same green shitty clothes? I ain't been happy one day, and that a lotta goddamn misery back to back in this ole boy. Is that Richie a good punk? Huh? Is he? He takes care of you and Roger—that how come you in this room, the three of you?

BILLY What?

CARLYLE *(Emphatically)* You and Roger are hittin' on Richie, right?

BILLY He's not queer, if that's what you're sayin'. A little effeminate, but that's all, no more; if that's what you're sayin'.

CARLYLE I'd like to get some of him myself if he a good punk, is what I'm sayin'. That's what I'm sayin'! You don't got no understandin' how a man can maybe be a little diplomatic about what he's sayin' sorta sideways, do you? Jesus.

BILLY He don't do that stuff.

CARLYLE *(Lying there)* What stuff?

BILLY Listen, man. I don't feel too good, you don't mind.

CARLYLE What stuff?

BILLY What you're thinkin'.

CARLYLE What . . . am I thinkin'?

BILLY You . . . know.

CARLYLE Yes, I do. It in my head, that how come I know. But how do you know? I can see your heart, Billy boy, but you cannot see mine. I am unknown. You . . . are known.

BILLY *(As if he is about to vomit, and fighting it)* You just . . . talk fast and keep movin', don't you? Don't ever stay still.

CARLYLE Words to say my feelin', Billy boy.
   (RICHIE steps into the room. He sees BILLY and CARLYLE, and freezes.)
   There he is. There he be.
   (RICHIE moves to his locker to put away the towel.)

RICHIE He's one of them who hasn't come down far out of the trees yet, Billy; believe me.

CARLYLE You got rudeness in your voice, Richie—you got meanness I can hear about ole Carlyle. You tellin' me I oughta leave—is that what you think you're doin'? You don't want me here?

RICHIE You come to see Roger, who isn't here, right? Man like you must have important matters to take care of all over the quad; I can't imagine a man like you not having extremely important things to do all over the world, as a matter of fact, Carlyle.

CARLYLE *(He rises. He begins to smooth the sheets and straighten the pillow. He will put the pint bottle in his back*

pocket and cross near to RICHIE.) Ohhhh, listen—don't mind
all the shit I say. I just talk bad, is all I do; I don't do bad.
I got to have friends just like anybody else. I'm just bored
and restless, that all; takin' it out on you two. I mean, I
know Richie here ain't really no punk, not really. I was just
talkin', just jivin' and entertainin' my own self. Don't take
me serious, not ever. I get on out and see you all later.
   (*He moves for the door,* RICHIE *right behind him, almost
   ushering him.*)
You be cool, hear? Man don't do the jivin', he the one
gettin' jived. That what my little brother Henry tell me
and tell me.
   (*Moving leisurely, he backs out the door and is gone.*
   RICHIE *shuts the door. There is a silence as* RICHIE *stands
   by the door.* BILLY *looks at him and then looks away.*)

BILLY I am gonna have to move myself outa here, Roger de-
cides to adopt that sonofabitch.

RICHIE He's an animal.

BILLY Yeh, and on top a that, he's a rotten person.

RICHIE (*He laughs nervously, crossing nearer to* BILLY.) I think
you're probably right.
   (*Still laughing a little, he pats* BILLY'S *shoulder and* BILLY
   freezes at the touch. Awkwardly RICHIE *removes his hand
   and crosses to his bed. When he has lain down,* BILLY
   *bends to take off his sneakers, then lies back on his pillow
   staring, thinking, and there is a silence.* RICHIE *does not
   move. He lies there, struggling to prepare himself for
   something.*)
Hey . . . Billy?
   (*Very slight pause*)
Billy?

BILLY Yeh.

RICHIE You know that story you told the other night?

BILLY Yeh . . . ?

RICHIE You know . . .

BILLY What . . . about it?

RICHIE Well, was it . . . about you?
  (Pause)
  I mean, was it . . . ABOUT you? Were you Frankie?
  (This is difficult for him.)
  Are . . . you Frankie? Billy?
  *(**BILLY** is slowly sitting up.)*

BILLY You sonofabitch . . . !

RICHIE Or was it really about somebody you knew . . . ?

BILLY *(Sitting, outraged and glaring)* You didn't hear me at all!

RICHIE I'm just asking a simple question, Billy, that's all I'm doing.

BILLY You are really sick. You know that? Your brain is really, truly rancid! Do you know there's a theory now it's genetic? That it's all a matter of genes and shit like that?

RICHIE Everything is not so ungodly cryptic, Billy.

BILLY You. You, man, and the rot it's makin' outa your feeble fuckin' brain.
  *(**ROGER**, dressed in civilian clothes, bursts in and **BILLY** leaps to his feet.)*

ROGER Hey, hey, anyone got a couple bucks he can loan me?

BILLY Rog, where you been?

ROGER *(Throwing the basketball and his sweat clothes into his locker)* I need five. C'mon.

BILLY Where you been? That asshole friend a yours was here.

ROGER I know, I know. Can you gimme five?

RICHIE *(He jumps to the floor and heads for his locker.)* You want five. I got it. You want ten or more, even?
(BILLY, watching RICHIE, turns, and nervously paces down right, where he moves about, worried.)

BILLY I mean, we gotta talk about him, man; we gotta talk about him.

ROGER *(As RICHIE is handing him two fives)* 'Cause we goin' to town together. I jus' run into him out on the quad, man, and he was feelin' real bad 'bout the way he acted, how you guys done him, he was fallin' down apologizin' all over the place.

BILLY *(As RICHIE marches back to his bed and sits down)* I mean, he's got a lotta weird ideas about us; I'm tellin' you.

ROGER He's just a little fucked up in his head is all, but he ain't trouble.
(He takes a pair of sunglasses from the locker and puts them on.)

BILLY Who needs him? I mean, we don't need him.

ROGER You gettin' too nervous, man. Nobody said anything about anybody needin' anybody. I been on the street all my life; he brings back home. I played me a little ball, Billy; took me a shower. I'm feelin' good!
(He has moved down to BILLY.)

BILLY I'm tellin' you there's something wrong with him, though.

ROGER *(Face to face with* BILLY, ROGER *is a little irritated.)* Every black man in the world ain't like me, man; you get used to that idea. You get to know him, and you gonna like him. I'm tellin' you. You get to be laughin' just like me to hear him talk his shit. But you gotta relax.

RICHIE I agree with Billy, Roger.

ROGER Well, you guys got it all worked out and that's good, but I am goin' to town with him. Man's got wheels. Got a good head. You got any sense, you'll come with us.

BILLY What are you talkin' about—come with you? I just tole you he's crazy.

ROGER And I tole you you're wrong.

RICHIE We weren't invited.

ROGER I'm invitin' you.

RICHIE No, I don't wanna.

ROGER *(He moves to* RICHIE; *it seems he really wants* RICHIE *to go.)* You sure, Richie? C'mon.

RICHIE No.

ROGER Billy? He got wheels, we goin' in drinkin', see if gettin' our heads real bad don't just make us feel real good. You know what I mean. I got him right; you got him wrong.

BILLY But what if I'm right?

ROGER Billy, Billy, the man is waitin' on me. You know you wanna. Jesus. Bad cat like that gotta know the way. He been to D.C. before. Got cousins here. Got wheels for the weekend. You always talkin' how you don't do nothin'—you just talk it. Let's do it tonight—stop talkin'. Be cruisin' up and down the strip, leanin' out the window, bad as we wanna be. True cool is a car. We can flip a cigarette out the window—we can watch it bounce. Get us some chippies. You know we can. And if we don't, he knows a cathouse, it fulla cats.

BILLY You serious?

RICHIE You mean you're going to a whorehouse? That's disgusting.

BILLY Listen who's talkin'. What do you want me to do? Stay here with you?

RICHIE We could go to a movie or something.

ROGER I am done with this talkin'. You goin', you stayin'?
(He crosses to his locker, pulls into view a wide-brimmed black and shiny hat, and puts it on, cocking it at a sharp angle.)

BILLY I don't know.

ROGER *(Stepping for the door)* I am goin'.

BILLY *(Turning, BILLY sees the hat.)* I'm going. Okay! I'm going! Going, going, going!
(And he runs to his locker.)

RICHIE Oh, Billy, you'll be scared to death in a cathouse and you know it.

BILLY BULLSHIT!
(He is removing his sweat pants and putting on a pair of gray corduroy trousers.)

ROGER Billy got him a lion-tamer 'tween his legs!
(The door bangs open and CARLYLE is there, still clad in his filthy fatigues, but wearing a going-to-town black knit cap on his head and carrying a bottle.)

CARLYLE Man, what's goin' on? I been waitin' like throughout my fuckin' life.

ROGER Billy's goin', too. He's gotta change.

CARLYLE He goin', too! Hey! Beautiful! That beautiful!
  (His grin is large, his laugh is loud.)

ROGER Didn't I tell you, Billy?

CARLYLE That beautiful, man; we all goin' to be friends!

RICHIE *(Sitting on his bed)* What about me, Carlyle?
  (CARLYLE looks at RICHIE, and then at ROGER and then he and ROGER begin to laugh. CARLYLE pokes ROGER and they laugh as they are leaving. BILLY, grabbing up his sneakers to follow, stops at the door, looking only briefly at RICHIE. Then BILLY goes and shuts the door. The lights are fading to black.)

S C E N E 2

In the dark, taps begins to play. And then slowly the lights rise, but the room remains dim. Only the lamp attached to RICHIE'S bed burns and there is the glow and spill of the hallway coming through the transom. BILLY, CARLYLE, ROGER and RICHIE are sprawled about the room. BILLY, lying on his stomach, has his head at the foot of his bed, a half-empty bottle of beer dangling in his hand. He wears a blue oxford-cloth shirt and his sneakers lie beside his bed. ROGER, collapsed in his own bed, lies upon his back, his head also at the foot, a *Playboy* magazine covering his face and a half-empty bottle of beer in his hands, folded on his belly. Having removed his civilian shirt, he wears a white T-shirt. CARLYLE is lying on his belly on RICHIE'S bed, his head at the foot, and he is facing out.

RICHIE is sitting on the floor, resting against ROGER'S footlocker. He is wrapped in a blanket. Beside him is an unopened bottle of beer and a bottle opener.

They are all dreamy in the dimness as taps plays sadly on and then fades into silence. No one moves.

RICHIE I don't know where it was, but it wasn't here. And we were all in it—it felt like—but we all had different faces. After you guys left, I only dozed for a few minutes, so it couldn't have been long. Roger laughed a lot and Billy was taller. I don't remember all the details exactly, and even though we were the ones in it, I know it was about my father. He was a big man. I was six. He was a very big man when I was six and he went away, but I remember him. He started drinking and staying home making model airplanes and boats and paintings by the numbers. We had money from mom's family, so he was just home all the time. And then one day I was coming home from kindergarten, and as I was starting up the front walk he came out the door and he had these suitcases in his hands. He was leaving, see, sneaking out, and I'd caught him. We looked at each other and I just knew and I started crying. He yelled at me, "Don't you cry; don't you start crying." I tried to grab him and he pushed me down in the grass. And then he was gone. G-O-N-E.

BILLY And that was it? That was it?

RICHIE I remember hiding my eyes. I lay in the grass and hid my eyes and waited.

BILLY He never came back?

RICHIE No.

CARLYLE Ain't that some shit. Now, I'm a jive-time street nigger. I knew where my daddy was all the while. He workin' in this butcher shop two blocks up the street. Ole Mom used to point him out. "There he go. That him—that your daddy." We'd see him on the street, "There he go."

ROGER Man couldn't see his way to livin' with you—that what you're sayin'?

CARLYLE Never saw the day.

ROGER And still couldn't get his ass outa the neighborhood?
(RICHIE begins trying to open his bottle of beer.)

CARLYLE Ain't that a bitch. Poor ole bastard just duck his head—Mom pointin' at him—he git this real goddamn hangdog look like he don't know who we talkin' about and he walk a little faster. Why the hell he never move away I don't know, unless he was crazy. But I don't think so. He come up to me once—I was playin'. "Boy," he says, "I ain't your daddy. I ain't. Your momma's crazy." "Don't you be callin' my momma crazy, Daddy," I tole him. Poor ole thing didn't know what to do.

RICHIE *(Giving up; he can't get the beer open.)* Somebody open this for me? I can't get this open.
(BILLY seems about to move to help, but CARLYLE is quicker, rising a little on the bunk and reaching.)

CARLYLE Ole Carlyle get it.
(RICHIE slides along the floor until he can place the bottle in CARLYLE's outstretched hand.)

RICHIE Then there was this once—there was this TV documentary about these bums in San Francisco, this TV guy interviewing all these bums, and just for maybe ten seconds while he was talkin' . . .
(Smiling, CARLYLE hands RICHIE the opened bottle.)
. . . to this one bum, there was this other one in the back-

ground jumpin' around like he thought he was dancin' and wavin' his hat, and even though there wasn't anything about him like my father and I didn't really ever see his face at all, I just kept thinkin': That's him. My dad. He thinks he's dancin'.

(*They lie there in silence and suddenly, softly,* BILLY *giggles, and then he giggles a little more and louder.*)

BILLY Jesus!

RICHIE What?

BILLY That's ridiculous, Richie; sayin' that, thinkin' that. If it didn't look like him, it wasn't him, but you gotta be makin' up a story.

CARLYLE (*Shifting now for a more comfortable position, he moves his head to the pillow at the top of the bed.*) Richie first saw me, he didn't like me much nohow, but he thought it over now, he changed his way a thinkin'. I can see that clear. We gonna be one big happy family.

RICHIE Carlyle likes me, Billy; he thinks I'm pretty.

CARLYLE (*Sitting up a little to make his point clear*) No, I don't think you pretty. A broad is pretty. Punks ain't pretty. Punk—if he good-lookin'—is cute. You cute.

RICHIE He's gonna steal me right away, little Billy. You're so slow, Bill. I prefer a man who's decisive.

(*He is lying down now on the floor at the foot of his bed.*)

BILLY You just keep at it, you're gonna have us all believin' you are just what you say you are.

RICHIE Which is more than we can say for you.

(*Now* ROGER *rises on his elbow to light a cigarette.*)

BILLY Jive, jive.

RICHIE You're arrogant, Billy. So arrogant.

BILLY What are you—on the rag?

RICHIE Wouldn't it just bang your little balls if I were!

ROGER *(To* RICHIE*)* Hey, man. What's with you?

RICHIE Stupidity offends me; lies and ignorance offend me.

BILLY You know where we was? The three of us? All three of us, earlier on? To the wrong side of the tracks, Richard. One good black upside-down whorehouse where you get what you buy, no jive along with it—so if it's a lay you want and need, you go! Or don't they have faggot whorehouses?

ROGER IF YOU GUYS DON'T CUT THIS SHIT OUT I'M GONNA BUST SOMEBODY'S HEAD!
   (Angrily he flops back on his bed. There is a silence as they all lie there.)

RICHIE "Where we was," he says. Listen to him. "Where we was." And he's got more school, Carlyle, than you have fingers and . . .
   (He has lifted his foot onto the bed; it touches, presses, CARLYLE'S *foot.)*
   . . . toes. It's this pseudo-earthy quality he feigns—but inside he's all cashmere.

BILLY That's a lie.
   (Giggling, he is staring at the floor.)
   I'm polyester, worsted and mohair.

RICHIE You have a lot of school, Billy; don't say you don't.

BILLY You said "fingers and toes"; you didn't say "a lot."

CARLYLE I think people get dumber the more they put their butts into some schoolhouse door.

BILLY It depends on what the hell you're talkin' about.
(*Now he looks at* CARLYLE, *and sees the feet touching.*)

CARLYLE I seen cats back on the block, they knew what was shakin'—then they got into all this school jive and, man, every year they went, they come back they didn't know nothin'.
(BILLY *is staring at* RICHIE'S *foot pressed and rubbing* CARLYLE'S *foot.* RICHIE *sees* BILLY *looking.* BILLY *cannot believe what he is seeing. It fills him with fear. The silence goes on and on.*)

RICHIE Billy, why don't you and Roger go for a walk?

BILLY What?
(*He bolts to his knees. He is frozen on his knees on the bed.*)

RICHIE Roger asked you to go downtown, you went, you had fun.

ROGER (*Having turned, he knows almost instantly what is going on.*) I asked you, too.

RICHIE You asked me; you *begged* Billy. I said no. Billy said no. You took my ten dollars. You begged Billy. I'm asking you a favor now—go for a walk. Let Carlyle and me have some time.
(*Silence*)

CARLYLE (*He sits up, uneasy and wary.*) That how you work it?

ROGER Work what?

CARLYLE Whosever turn it be.

BILLY No, no, that ain't the way we work it, because *we don't work it.*

CARLYLE See? See? There it is—that goddamn education showin' through. All them years in school. Man, didn't we have a good time tonight? You rode in my car. I showed you a good cathouse, all that sweet black pussy. Ain't we friends? Richie likes me. How come you don't like me?

BILLY 'Cause if you really are doin' what I think you're doin', you're a fuckin' animal!
(CARLYLE *leaps to his feet, hand snaking to his pocket to draw a weapon.*)

ROGER Billy, no.

BILLY NO, WHAT?!

ROGER Relax, man; no need.
(*He turns to* CARLYLE; *patiently, wearily, he speaks.*)
Man, I tole you it ain't goin' on here. We both tole you it ain't goin' on here.

CARLYLE Don't you jive me, nigger. You goin' for a walk like I'm askin', or not? I wanna get this clear.

ROGER Man, we live here.

RICHIE It's my house, too, Roger; I live here, too.
(RICHIE *bounds to his feet, flinging the blanket that has been covering him so it flies and lands on the floor near* ROGER'S *footlocker.*)

ROGER Don't I know that? Did I say somethin' to make you think I didn't know that?
(*Standing,* RICHIE *is removing his trousers and throwing them down on his footlocker.*)

RICHIE Carlyle is my guest.
(*Sitting down on the side of his bed and facing out, he puts his arms around* CARLYLE'S *thigh.* ROGER *jumps to*

his feet and grabs the blanket from the foot of his bed. Shaking it open, he drops onto the bed, his head at the foot of the bed and facing off as he covers himself.)

ROGER Fine. He your friend. This your home. So that mean he can stay. It don't mean I gotta leave. I'll catch you all in the mornin'.

BILLY Roger, what the hell are you doin'?

ROGER What you better do, Billy. It's gettin' late. I'm goin' to sleep.

BILLY What?

ROGER Go to fucking bed, Billy. Get up in the rack, turn your back and look at the wall.

BILLY You gotta be kiddin'.

ROGER DO IT!

BILLY Man ...!

ROGER Yeah ...!

BILLY You mean just ...

ROGER It been goin' on a long damn time, man. You ain't gonna put no stop to it.

CARLYLE You ... ain't ... serious.

RICHIE *(Both he and* CARLYLE *are staring at* ROGER *and then* BILLY, *who is staring at* ROGER.*)* Well, I don't believe it. Of all the childish ... infantile ...

CARLYLE Hey!
    (Silence)
    HEY! Even I got to say this is a little weird, but if this the way you do it ...

(And he turns toward RICHIE *below him.)*
. . . it the way I do it. I don't know.

RICHIE With them right there? Are you kidding? My God,
Carlyle, that'd be obscene.
(Pulling slightly away from CARLYLE*)*

CARLYLE Ohhh, man . . . they backs turned.

RICHIE No.

CARLYLE What I'm gonna do?
(Silence. He looks at them, all three of them.)
Don't you got no feelin' for how a man feel? I don't under-
stand you two boys. Unless'n you a pair of motherfuckers.
That what you are, you a pair of motherfuckers? You slits,
man. DON'T YOU HEAR ME!? I DON'T UNDERSTAND THIS SITUA-
TION HERE. I THOUGHT WE MADE A DEAL!
*(*RICHIE *rises, starts to pull on his trousers.* CARLYLE *grabs
him.)*
YOU GET ON YOUR KNEES, YOU PUNK, I MEAN NOW, AND YOU
GONNA BE ON MY JOINT FAST OR YOU GONNA BE ONE BUSTED
PUNK. AM I UNDERSTOOD?
(He hurls RICHIE *down to the floor.)*

BILLY I ain't gonna have this going on here; Roger, I can't.

ROGER I been turnin' my back on one thing or another all my
life.

RICHIE Jealous, Billy?

BILLY *(Getting to his feet)* Just go out that door, the two of
you. Go. Go on out in the bushes or out in some field. See
if I follow you. See if I care. I'll be right here and I'll be
sleepin', but it ain't gonna be done in my house. I don't
have much in this goddamn army, but *here* is mine.
(He stands beside his bed.)

CARLYLE I WANT MY FUCKIN' NUT! HOW COME YOU SO UPTIGHT? HE WANTS ME! THIS BOY HERE WANTS ME! WHO YOU TO STOP IT?

ROGER *(Spinning to face* CARLYLE *and* RICHIE) That's right, Billy. Richie one a those people want to get fucked by niggers, man. It what he know was gonna happen all his life—can be his dream come true. Ain't that right, Richie!
(Jumping to his feet, RICHIE *starts putting on his trousers.)* Want to make it real in the world, how a nigger is an animal. Give 'em an inch, gonna take a mile. Ain't you some kinda fool, Richie? Hear me, Carlyle.

CARLYLE Man, don't make me no nevermind what he think he's provin' an' shit, long as I get my nut. I KNOW I ain't no animal, don't have to prove it.

RICHIE *(Pulling at* CARLYLE'S *arm, wanting to move him toward the door)* Let's go. Let's go outside. The hell with it.
(But CARLYLE *tears himself free; he squats furiously down on the bunk, his hands seizing it, his back to all of them.)*

CARLYLE Bull shit. Bullshit! I ain't goin' no-fuckin'-where—this jive ass ain't runnin' me. Is this you house or not?
(He doesn't know what is going on; he can hardly look at any of them.)

ROGER *(Bounding out of bed, hurling his pillow across the room)* I'm goin' to the fuckin' john, Billy. Hang it up, man; let 'em be.

BILLY No.

ROGER I'm smarter than you—do like I'm sayin'.

BILLY It ain't right.

ROGER Who gives a big rat's ass!

CARLYLE Right on, bro! That boy know; he do.
(He circles the bed toward them.)
Hear him. Look into his eyes.

BILLY This fuckin' army takin' everything else away from me, they ain't takin' more than they got. I see what I see—I don't run, don't hide.

ROGER *(Turning away from* BILLY, *he stomps out the door, slamming it.)* You fuckin' well better learn.

CARLYLE That right. Time for more schoolin'. Lesson number one.
(Stealthily he steps and snaps out the only light, the lamp clamped to RICHIE's *bed.)*
You don't see what you see so well in the dark. It dark in the night. Black man got a black body—he disappear.
(The darkness is so total they are all no more than shadows.)

RICHIE Not to the hands; not to the fingers.
(Moving from across the room toward CARLYLE*)*

CARLYLE You do like you talk, boy, you gonna make me happy.
(As BILLY, *nervously clutching his sneaker, is moving backward.)*

BILLY Who says the lights go out? Nobody goddamn asked me if the lights go out.
*(*BILLY, *lunging to the wall switch, throws it. The overhead lights flash on, flooding the room with light.* CARLYLE *is seated on the edge of* RICHIE's *bed,* RICHIE *kneeling before him.)*

CARLYLE I DO, MOTHERFUCKER, I SAY!
(And the switchblade seems to leap from his pocket to his hand.)
I SAY! CAN'T YOU LET PEOPLE BE?

(BILLY hurls his sneaker at the floor at CARLYLE's feet. Instantly CARLYLE is across the room, blocking BILLY's escape out the door.)

Goddamn you, boy! I'm gonna cut your ass, just to show you how it feel—and cuttin' can happen. This knife true.

RICHIE Carlyle, now c'mon.

CARLYLE Shut up, pussy.

RICHIE Don't hurt him, for chrissake.

CARLYLE Goddamn man throw a shoe at me, he don't walk around clean in the world thinkin' he can throw another. He get some shit come back at him.

(BILLY doesn't know which way to go, and then CARLYLE, jabbing the knife at the air before BILLY's chest, has BILLY running backward, his eyes fixed on the moving blade. He stumbles, having run into RICHIE's bed. He sprawls backward and CARLYLE is over him.)

No, no; no, no. Put you hand out there. Put it out.

(Slight pause; BILLY is terrified.)

DO THE THING I'M TELLIN'!

(BILLY lets his hand rise in the air and CARLYLE grabs it, holds it.)

That's it. That's good. See? See?

(The knife flashes across BILLY's palm; the blood flows. BILLY winces, recoils, but CARLYLE's hand still clenches and holds.)

BILLY Motherfucker.

(Again the knife darts, cutting, and BILLY yelps. RICHIE, on his knees beside them, turns away.)

RICHIE Oh, my God, what are you—

CARLYLE *(In his own sudden distress, CARLYLE flings the hand away.)* That you blood. The blood inside you, you don't ever see it there. Take a look how easy it come out—and enough of it come out, you in the middle of the worst god-damn trouble you ever gonna see. And know I'm the man can deal that kinda trouble, easy as I smile. And I smile . . . easy. Yeah.

(BILLY *is curled in upon himself, holding the hand to his* stomach as RICHIE *now reaches tentatively and shyly out as if to console* BILLY, *who repulses the gesture.* CARLYLE *is angry and strangely depressed. Forlornly he slumps onto* BILLY'S *footlocker as* BILLY *staggers up to his wall locker and takes out a towel.)*

Bastard ruin my mood, Richie. He ruin my mood. Fightin' and lovin' real different in the feelin's I got. I see blood come outa somebody like that, it don't make me feel good —hurt me—hurt on somebody I thought was my friend. But I ain't supposed to see. One dumb nigger. No mind, he thinks, no heart, no feelings a gentleness. You see how that ain't true, Richie. Goddamn man threw a shoe at me. A lotta people woulda cut his heart out. I gotta make him know he throw shit, he get shit. But I don't hurt him bad, you see what I mean?

(BILLY'S *back is to them, as he stands hunched at his locker, and suddenly his voice, hissing, erupts.)*

BILLY Jesus . . . H. . . . Christ . . . ! Do you know what I'm doin'? Do you know what I'm standin' here doin'?

(He whirls now; he holds a straight razor in his hand. A bloody towel is wrapped around the hurt hand. CARLYLE tenses, rises, seeing the razor.)

I'm a twenty-four-year-old goddamn college graduate—intel-lectual goddamn scholar type—and I got a razor in my hand. I'm thinkin' about comin' up behind one black human being and I'm thinkin' nigger this and nigger that—I wanna cut his throat. THAT IS RIDICULOUS. I NEVER FACED ANYBODY

IN MY LIFE WITH ANYTHING TO KILL THEM. YOU UNDERSTAND ME? I DON'T HAVE A GODDAMN THING ON THE LINE HERE!

(The door opens and ROGER *rushes in, having heard the yelling.* BILLY *flings the razor into his locker.)*

Look at me, Roger, look at me. I got a cut palm—I don't know what happened. Jesus Christ, I got sweat all over me when I think a what I was near to doin'. I swear it. I mean, do I think I need a reputation as a killer, a bad man with a knife?

(He is wild with the energy of feeling free and with the anger at what these others almost made him do. CARLYLE *slumps down on the footlocker; he sits there.)*

Bullshit! I need shit! I got sweat all over me. I got the mile record in my hometown. I did four forty-two in high school and that's the goddamn record in Windsor County. I don't need approval from either one of the pair of you.

(And he rushes at RICHIE.*)*

You wanna be a goddamn swish—a goddamn faggot-queer —GO! Suckin' cocks and takin' it in the ass, the thing of which you dream—GO! AND YOU—

(Whirling on CARLYLE*)*

You wanna be a bad-assed animal, man, get it on—go—but I wash my hands. I am not human as you are. I put you down, I put you down—

(He almost hurls himself at RICHIE.*)*

—you gay little piece a shit cake—SHIT CAKE. AND YOU—

(Hurt, confused, RICHIE *turns away, nearly pressing his face into the bed beside which he kneels, as* BILLY *has spun back to tower over the pulsing, weary* CARLYLE.*)*

—you are your own goddamn fault, SAMBO! SAMBO!

(And the knife flashes up in CARLYLE's *hand into* BILLY's *stomach, and* BILLY *yelps.)*

Ahhhhhhhhh.

(And pushes at the hand. RICHIE *is still turned away.)*

RICHIE Well, fuck you, Billy.

BILLY *(He backs off the knife.)* Get away, get away.

RICHIE *(As* ROGER, *who could not see because* BILLY'S *back is to him, is approaching* CARLYLE *and* BILLY *goes walking up toward the lockers as if he knows where he is going, as if he is going to go out the door and to a movie, his hands holding his belly)* You're so-o messed up.

ROGER *(To* CARLYLE*)* Man, what's the matter with you?

CARLYLE Don't nobody talk that weird shit to me, you understand?

ROGER You jive, man. That's all you do—jive!
*(*BILLY, *striding swiftly, walks flat into the wall lockers; he bounces, turns. They are all looking at him.)*

RICHIE Billy! Oh, Billy!
*(*ROGER *looks at* RICHIE.*)*

BILLY Ahhhhhhh. Ahhhhhhh.
*(*ROGER *looks at* CARLYLE *as if he is about to scream, and beyond him,* BILLY *turns from the lockers, starts to walk again, now staggering and moving toward them.)*

RICHIE I think . . . he stabbed him. I think Carlyle stabbed Billy. Roger!
*(*ROGER *whirls to go to* BILLY, *who is staggering downstage and angled away, hands clenched over his belly.)*

BILLY Shut up! It's just a cut, it's just a cut. He cut my hand, he cut gut.
(He collapses onto his knees just beyond ROGER'S *footlocker.)*
It took the wind out of me, scared me, that's all.
(Fiercely he tries to hide the wound and remain calm.)

ROGER Man, are you all right?
>(*He moves to* BILLY, *who turns to hide the wound. Till now no one is sure what happened.* RICHIE *only "thinks"* BILLY *has been stabbed.* BILLY *is pretending he isn't hurt. As* BILLY *turns from* ROGER, *he turns toward* RICHIE *and* RICHIE *sees the blood.* RICHIE *yelps and they all begin talking and yelling simultaneously.*)

CARLYLE You know what I was learnin', he was learnin' to talk all that weird shit, cuttin', baby, cuttin', the ways and means a shit, man, razors.

ROGER You all right? Or what? He slit you?

BILLY Just took the wind outa me, scared me.

RICHIE Carlyle, you stabbed him; you stabbed him.

CARLYLE Ohhhh, pussy, pussy, pussy, Carlyle know what he do.

ROGER (*Trying to lift* BILLY) Get up, okay? Get up on the bed.

BILLY (*Irritated, pulling free*) I am on the bed.

ROGER What?

RICHIE No, Billy, no, you're not.

BILLY Shut up!

RICHIE You're on the floor.

BILLY I'm on the bed. I'm on the bed.
>(*Emphatically. And then he looks at the floor.*)
What?

ROGER Let me see what he did.
>(BILLY'S *hands are clenched on the wound.*)
Billy, let me see where he got you.

BILLY (*Recoiling*) NO-O-O-O-O-O, you nigger!

ROGER *(He leaps at* CARLYLE.*)* What did you do?

CARLYLE *(Hunching his shoulders, ducking his head)* Shut up.

ROGER What did you do, nigger—you slit him or stick him?
(And then he tries to get back to BILLY.*)*
Billy, let me see.

BILLY *(Doubling over till his head hits the floor)* NO-O-O-O-O-O!
Shit, shit, shit.

RICHIE *(Suddenly sobbing and yelling)* Oh, my God, my God,
ohhhh, ohhhh, ohhhh.
(Bouncing on his knees on the bed)

CARLYLE FUCK IT, FUCK IT, I STUCK HIM. I TURNED IT. This
mother army break my heart. I can't be out there where it
pretty, don't wanna live! Wash me clean, shit face!

RICHIE Ohhhh, ohhhh, ohhhhhhhhhhh. Carlyle stabbed
Billy, oh, ohhhh, I never saw such a thing in my life.
Ohhhhhh.
(As ROGER *is trying gently, fearfully, to straighten* BILLY *up)*
Don't die, Billy; don't die.

ROGER Shut up and go find somebody to help. Richie, go!

RICHIE Who? I'll go, I'll go.
(Scrambling off the bed)

ROGER I don't know. JESUS CHRIST! DO IT!

RICHIE Okay. Okay. Billy, don't die. Don't die.
(Backing for the door, he turns and runs.)

ROGER The sarge, or C.Q.

BILLY *(Suddenly doubling over, vomiting blood.* RICHIE *is
gone.)* Ohhhhhhhhhh. Blood. Blood.

ROGER Be still, be still.

BILLY *(Pulling at a blanket on the floor beside him)* I want to stand up. I'm——vomiting——
(Making no move to stand, only to cover himself)
——blood. What does that mean?

ROGER *(Slowly standing)* I don't know.

BILLY Yes, yes, I want to stand up. Give me blanket, blanket.
(He rolls back and forth, fighting to get the blanket over him.)

ROGER RIICCHHHIIIEEEE!
(As **BILLY** *is furiously grappling with the blanket)*
No, no.
(He looks at **CARLYLE,** *who is slumped over, muttering to himself.* **ROGER** *runs for the door.)*
Wait on, be tight, be cool.

BILLY Cover me. Cover me.
(At last he gets the blanket over his face. The dark makes him grow still. He lies there beneath his blanket. Silence. No one moves. And then **CARLYLE** *senses the quiet; he turns, looks. Slowly, wearily, he rises and walks to where* **BILLY** *lies. He stands over him, the knife hanging loosely from his left hand as he reaches with his right to gently take the blanket and lift it slowly from* **BILLY'S** *face. They look at each other.* **BILLY** *reaches up and pats* **CARLYLE'S** *hand holding the blanket.)*
I don't want to talk to you right now, Carlyle. All right? Where's Roger? Do you know where he is?
(Slight pause)
Don't stab me anymore, Carlyle, okay? I was dead wrong doin' what I did. I know that now. Carlyle, promise me you won't stab me anymore. I couldn't take it. Okay? I'm cold ... my blood ... is ...
(From off comes a voice.)

ROONEY Cokesy? Cokesy wokesy?
(*And* ROONEY *staggers into the doorway, very drunk, a beer bottle in his hand.*)
Ollie-ollie oxen-freeee.
(*He looks at them.* CARLYLE *quickly, secretly, slips the knife into his pocket.*)
How you all doin'? Everybody drunk, huh? I los' my friend.
(*He is staggering sideways toward* BILLY'S *bunk, where he finally drops down, sitting.*)
Who are you, soldier?
(CARLYLE *has straightened, his head ducked down as he is edging for the door.*)
Who are you, soldier?
(*And* RICHIE, *running, comes roaring into the room. He looks at* ROONEY *and cannot understand what is going on.* CARLYLE *is standing.* ROONEY *is just sitting there. What is going on?* RICHIE *moves along the lockers, trying to get behind* ROONEY, *his eyes never off* CARLYLE.)

RICHIE Ohhhhhh, Sergeant Rooney, I've been looking for you everywhere—where have you been? Carlyle stabbed Billy, he stabbed him.

ROONEY (*Sitting there*) What?

RICHIE Carlyle stabbed Billy.

ROONEY Who's Carlyle?

RICHIE He's Carlyle.
(*As* CARLYLE *seems about to advance, the knife again showing in his hand*)
Carlyle, don't hurt anybody more!

ROONEY (*On his feet, he is staggering toward the door.*) You got a knife there? What's with the knife? What's goin' on here?

(CARLYLE steps as if to bolt for the door, but ROONEY is in the way, having inserted himself between CARLYLE and RICHIE, who has backed into the doorway.)
Wait! Now wait!

RICHIE *(As CARLYLE raises the knife)* Carlyle, don't!
(RICHIE runs from the room.)

ROONEY You watch your step, you understand. You see what I got here?
(He lifts the beer bottle, waves it threateningly.)
You watch your step, motherfucker. Relax. I mean, we can straighten all this out. We—
(CARLYLE lunges at ROONEY, who tenses.)
I'm just askin' what's goin' on, that's all I'm doin'. No need to get all—
(And CARLYLE swipes at the air again; ROONEY recoils.)
Motherfucker. Motherfucker.
(He seems to be tensing, his body gathering itself for some mighty effort. And he throws his head back and gives the eagle yell.)
Eeeeeeeeeeeaaaaaaaaaaaaaaaaahhhhhhh! Eeeeaaaaaaaaaaaaah-hhhhhhhhhhhh!
(CARLYLE jumps; he looks left and right.)
Goddammit, I'll cut you good.
(He lunges to break the bottle on the edge of the wall lockers. The bottle shatters and he yelps, dropping everything.)
Ohhhhhhhh! Ohhhhhhhhhhhhhh!
(CARLYLE bolts, running from the room.)
I hurt myself, I cut myself. I hurt my hand.
(Holding the wounded hand, he scurries to BILLY'S bed, where he sits on the edge, trying to wipe the blood away so he can see the wound.)
I cut—

(Hearing a noise, he whirls, looks; CARLYLE *is plummeting in the door and toward him.* ROONEY *stands.)*
I hurt my hand, goddammit!
(The knife goes into ROONEY'S *belly. He flails at* CARLYLE.*)*
I HURT MY HAND! WHAT ARE YOU DOING? WHAT ARE YOU DOING? WAIT! WAIT!
(He turns away, falling to his knees, and the knife goes into him again and again.)
No fair. No fair!
*(*ROGER, *running, skids into the room, headed for* BILLY, *and then he sees* CARLYLE *on* ROONEY, *the leaping knife.* ROGER *lunges, grabbing* CARLYLE, *pulling him to get him off* ROONEY. CARLYLE *leaps free of* ROGER, *sending* ROGER *flying backward. And then* CARLYLE *begins to circle* ROGER'S *bed. He is whimpering, wiping at the blood on his shirt as if to wipe it away.* ROGER *backs away as* CARLYLE *keeps waving the knife at him.* ROONEY *is crawling along the floor under* BILLY'S *bed and then he stops crawling, lies there.)*

CARLYLE You don't tell nobody on me you saw me do this, I let you go, okay? Ohhhhhhhhh.
(Rubbing, rubbing at the shirt)
Ohhhhhh, how'm I gonna get back to the world now, I got all this mess to—

ROGER What happened? That you—I don't understand that you did this! That you did—

CARLYLE YOU SHUT UP! Don't be talkin' all that weird shit to me—don't you go talkin' all that weird shit!

ROGER Noooooooooooooo!

CARLYLE I'm Carlyle, man. You know me. You know me.
(He turns, he flees out the door. ROGER, *alone, looks about*

the room. BILLY *is there.* ROGER *moves toward* BILLY, *who is shifting, undulating on his back.)*

BILLY Carlyle, no; oh, Christ, don't stab me anymore. I'll die. I will—I'll die. Don't make me die. I'll get my dog after you. I'LL GET MY DOG AFTER YOU!
*(*ROGER *is saying, "Oh, Billy, man, Billy." He is trying to hold* BILLY. *Now he lifts* BILLY *into his arms.)*

ROGER Oh, Billy; oh, man. GODDAMMIT, BILLY!
(As a MILITARY POLICE LIEUTENANT *comes running in the door, his .45 automatic drawn, and he levels it at* ROGER*)*

LIEUTENANT Freeze, soldier! Not a quick move out of you. Just real slow, straighten your ass up.
*(*ROGER *has gone rigid; the* LIEUTENANT *is advancing on him. Tentatively* ROGER *turns, looks.)*

ROGER Huh? No.

LIEUTENANT Get your ass against the lockers.

ROGER Sir, no. I—

LIEUTENANT *(Hurling* ROGER *away toward the wall lockers)* MOVE!
(As another M.P., Pfc HINSON, *comes in, followed by* RICHIE, *flushed and breathless)*
Hinson, cover this bastard.

HINSON *(Drawing his .45 automatic, moving on* ROGER*)* Yes, sir.
(The LIEUTENANT *frisks* ROGER, *who is spread-eagled at the lockers.)*

RICHIE What? Oh, sir, no, no. Roger, what's going on?

LIEUTENANT I'll straighten this shit out.

ROGER Tell 'em to get the gun off me, Richie.

LIEUTENANT SHUT UP!

RICHIE But, sir, sir, he didn't do it. Not him.

LIEUTENANT *(Fiercely he shoves* RICHIE *out of the way.)* I told
you, all of you, to shut up.
   (He moves to ROONEY'S *body.)*
Jesus, God, this Sfc is cut to shit. He's cut to shit.
   (He hurries to BILLY'S *body.)*
This man is cut to shit.
   (As CARLYLE *appears in the doorway, his hands cuffed
   behind him, a third M.P., Pfc* CLARK, *shoving him for-
   ward.* CARLYLE *seems shocked and cunning, his mind
   whirring.)*

CLARK Sir, I got this guy on the street, runnin' like a streak a
shit.
   (He hurls the struggling CARLYLE *forward and* CARLYLE
   stumbles toward the head of RICHIE'S *bed as* RICHIE, *seeing
   him coming, hurries away along* BILLY'S *bed and toward
   the wall lockers.)*

RICHIE He did it! Him, him!

CARLYLE What is going on here? I don't know what is going
on here!

CLARK *(Club at the ready, he stations himself beside* CARLYLE.*)*
He's got blood all over him, sir. All over him.

LIEUTENANT What about the knife?

CLARK No, sir. he must have thrown it away.
   *(As a fourth M.P. has entered to stand in the doorway,
   and* HINSON, *leaving* ROGER, *bends to examine* ROONEY.
   He will also kneel and look for life in BILLY.*)*

LIEUTENANT You throw it away, soldier?

CARLYLE Oh, you thinkin' about how my sister got happened, too. Oh, you ain't so smart as you think you are! No way!

ROGER Jesus God almighty.

LIEUTENANT What happened here? I want to know what happened here.

HINSON (Rising from BILLY's body) They're both dead, sir. Both of them.

LIEUTENANT (Confidential, almost whispering) I know they're both dead. That's what I'm talkin' about.

CARLYLE Chicken blood, sir. Chicken blood and chicken hearts is what all over me. I was goin' on my way, these people jump out the bushes be pourin' it all over me. Chicken blood and chicken hearts.
(Thrusting his hands out at CLARK)
You goin' take these cuffs off me, boy?

LIEUTENANT Sit him down, Clark. Sit him down and shut him up.

CARLYLE This my house, sir. This my goddamn house.
(CLARK grabs him, begins to move him.)

LIEUTENANT I said to shut him up.

CLARK Move it; move!
(Struggling to get CARLYLE over to ROGER's footlocker as HINSON and the other M.P. exit)

CARLYLE I want these cuffs taken off my hands.

CLARK You better do like you been told. You better sit and shut up!

CARLYLE I'm gonna be thinkin' over here. I'm gonna be thinkin' it all over. I got plannin' to do. I'm gonna be thinkin' in my quietness; don't you be makin' no mistake.

(He slumps over, muttering to himself. HINSON *and the other M.P. return, carrying a stretcher. They cross to* BILLY, *chatting with each other about how to go about the lift. They will lift him; they will carry him out.)*

LIEUTENANT *(To* RICHIE*)* You're Wilson?

RICHIE No, sir.
(Indicating BILLY*)*
That's Wilson. I'm Douglas.

LIEUTENANT *(To* ROGER*)* And you're Moore. And you sleep here.

ROGER Yes, sir.

RICHIE Yes, sir. And Billy slept here and Sergeant Rooney was our platoon sergeant and Carlyle was a transient, sir. He was a transient from P Company.

LIEUTENANT *(Scrutinizing* ROGER*)* And you had nothing to do with this?
(To RICHIE*)*
He had nothing to do with this?

ROGER No, sir, I didn't.

RICHIE No, sir, he didn't. I didn't either. Carlyle went crazy and he got into a fight and it was awful. I didn't even know what it was about exactly.

LIEUTENANT How'd the Sfc get involved?

RICHIE Well, he came in, sir.

ROGER I had to run off to call you, sir. I wasn't here.

RICHIE Sergeant Rooney just came in—I don't know why—he heard all the yelling, I guess—and Carlyle went after him. Billy was already stabbed.

CARLYLE *(Rising, his manner that of a man who is taking charge)* All right now, you gotta be gettin' the fuck outa here. All of you. I have decided enough of the shit has been goin' on around here and I am tellin' you to be gettin' these motherfuckin' cuffs off me and you be gettin' me a bus ticket home. I am quittin' this jive-time army.

LIEUTENANT You are doin' what?

CARLYLE No, I ain't gonna be quiet. No way. I am quittin' this goddamn—

LIEUTENANT You shut the hell up, soldier. I am ordering you.

CARLYLE I don't understand you people! Don't you people understand when a man be talkin' English at you to say his mind? I have quit the army!
  (As HINSON returns)

LIEUTENANT Get him outa here!

RICHIE What's the matter with him?

LIEUTENANT Hinson! Clark!
  (They move, grabbing CARLYLE, and they drag him, struggling, toward the door.)

CARLYLE Oh, no. Oh, no. You ain't gonna be doin' me no more. I been tellin' you. To get away from me. I am stayin' here. This my place, not your place. You take these cuffs off me like I been tellin' you! My poor little sister Lin Sue understood what was goin' on here! She tole me! She knew!
  (He is howling in the hallway now.)
You better be gettin' these cuffs off me!
  (Silence. ROGER, RICHIE and the LIEUTENANT are all staring at the door. The LIEUTENANT turns, crosses to the foot of ROGER's bed.)

LIEUTENANT All right now. I will be getting to the bottom of this. You know I will be getting to the bottom of this.
(He is taking two forms from his clipboard.)

RICHIE Yes, sir.
*(*HINSON* and the fourth M.P. return with another stretcher. They walk to *ROONEY*, talking to one another about how to lift him. They drag him from under the bed. They will roll him onto the stretcher, lift him and walk out. *ROGER* moves, watching them, down along the edge of *BILLY'S* bed.)*

LIEUTENANT Fill out these forms. I want your serial number, rank, your MOS, the NCOIC of your work. Any leave coming up will be canceled. Tomorrow at o8oo you will report to my office at the provost marshal's headquarters. You know where that is?

ROGER *(As the two M.P.'s are leaving with the stretcher and* ROONEY'S *body)* Yes, sir.

RICHIE Yes, sir.

LIEUTENANT *(Crossing to* ROGER, *he hands him two cards.)* Be prepared to do some talking. Two perfectly trained and primed strong pieces of U.S. Army property got cut to shit up here. We are going to find out how and why. Is that clear?

RICHIE Yes, sir.

ROGER Yes, sir.
(The LIEUTENANT *looks at each of them. He surveys the room. He marches out.)*

RICHIE Oh, my God. Oh. Oh.
(He runs to his bed and collapses, sitting hunched down at the foot. He holds himself and rocks as if very cold.

ROGER, *quietly, is weeping. He stands and then walks to his bed. He puts down the two cards. He moves purposefully up to the mops hanging on the wall in the corner. He takes one down. He moves with the mop and the bucket to* BILLY'S *bed, where* ROONEY'S *blood stains the floor. He mops.* RICHIE, *in horror, is watching.)*

RICHIE What . . . are you doing?

ROGER This area a mess, man.
(Dragging the bucket, carrying the mop, he moves to the spot where BILLY *had lain. He begins to mop.)*

RICHIE That's Billy's blood, Roger. His blood.

ROGER Is it?

RICHIE I feel awful.

ROGER *(He keeps mopping.)* How come you made me waste all that time talkin' shit to you, Richie? All my time talkin' shit, and all the time you was a faggot, man; you really was. You shoulda jus' tole ole Roger. He don't care. All you gotta do is tell me.

RICHIE I've been telling you. I did.

ROGER Jive, man, jive!

RICHIE No!

ROGER You did bullshit all over us! ALL OVER US!

RICHIE I just wanted to hold his hand, Billy's hand, to talk to him, go to the movies hand in hand like he would with a girl or I would with someone back home.

ROGER But he didn't wanna; *he* didn't wanna.
(Finished now, ROGER *drags the mop and bucket back toward the corner.* RICHIE *is sobbing; he is at the edge of hysteria.)*

RICHIE He did.

ROGER No, man.

RICHIE He did. He did. It's not my fault.
(ROGER *slams the bucket into the corner and rams the* *mop into the bucket. Furious, he marches down to* RICHIE. *Behind him* SERGEANT COKES, *grinning and lifting a wine bottle, appears in the doorway.*)

COKES Hey!
(RICHIE, *in despair, rolls onto his belly.* COKES *is very, very happy.*)
Hey! What a day, gen'l'men. How you all doin'?

ROGER (*Crossing up near the head of his own bed*) Hello, Sergeant Cokes.

COKES (*Affectionate and casual, he moves near to* ROGER.) How you all doin'? Where's ole Rooney? I lost him.

ROGER What?

COKES We had a hell of a day, ole Rooney and me, lemme tell you. We been playin' hide-and-go-seek, and I was hidin', and now I think maybe he started hidin' without tellin' me he was gonna and I can't find him and I thought maybe he was hidin' up here.

RICHIE Sergeant, he—

ROGER No. No, we ain't seen him.

COKES I gotta find him. He knows how to react in a tough situation. He didn't come up here looking for me?
(ROGER *moves around to the far side of his bed, turning his back to* COKES. *Sitting,* ROGER *takes out a cigarette, but he does not light it.*)

ROGER We was goin' to sleep, Sarge. Got to get up early. You know the way this mother army is.

COKES *(Nodding, drifting backward, he sits down on* BILLY'S *bed.)* You don't mind I sit here a little. Wait on him. Got a little wine. You can have some.
    (Tilting his head way back, he takes a big drink and then, looking straight ahead, corks the bottle with a whack of his hand.)
We got back into the area—we had been downtown—he wanted to play hide-and-go-seek. I tole him okay, I was ready for that. He hid his eyes. So I run and hid in the bushes and then under this Jeep. 'Cause I thought it was better. I hid and I hid and I hid. He never did come. So finally, I got tired—I figured I'd give up, come lookin' for him. I was way over by the movie theater. I don't know how I got there. Anyway, I got back here and I figured maybe he come up here lookin' for me, figurin' I was hidin' up with you guys. You ain't seen him, huh?

ROGER No, we ain't seen him. I tole you that, Sarge.

COKES Oh.

RICHIE Roger!

ROGER He's drunk, Richie! He's blasted drunk. Got a brain turned to mush!

COKES *(In deep agreement)* That ain't no lie.

ROGER Let it be for the night, Richie. Let him be for the night.

COKES I still know what's goin' on, though. Never no worry about that. I always know what's goin' on. I always know. Don't matter what I drink or how much I drink. I always

still know what's goin' on. But . . . I'll be goin' maybe and
look for Rooney.

(But rising, he wanders down center.)

But . . . I mean, we could be doin' that forever. Him and
me. Me under the Jeep. He wants to find me, he goes to the
Jeep. I'm over here. He comes here. I'm gone. You know,
maybe I'll just wait a little while more I'm here. He'll find
me then if he comes here. You guys want another drink.

(Turning, he goes to BILLY's footlocker, where he sits and
takes another enormous guzzle of wine.)

Jesus, what a goddamn day we had. Me and Rooney started
drivin' and we was comin' to this intersection and out comes
this goddamn Chevy. I try to get around her, but no dice.
BINGO! I hit her in the left rear. She was furious. I didn't
care. I gave her my name and number. My car had a head-
light out, the fender bashed in. Rooney wouldn't stop
laughin'. I didn't know what to do. So we went to D.C. to
this private club I know. Had ten or more snorts and decided to get back here after playin' some snooker. That was
fun. On the way, we picked up this kid from the engineering
unit, hitchhiking. I'm starting to feel real clear-headed now.
So I'm comin' around this corner and all of a sudden there's
this car stopped dead in front of me. He's not blinkin' to
turn or anything. I slam on the brakes, but it's like puddin'
the way I slide into him. There's a big noise and we yell.
Rooney starts laughin' like crazy and the kid jumps outa the
back and says he's gonna take a fuckin' bus. The guy from
the other car is swearin' at me. My car's still workin' fine,
so I move it off to the side and tell him to do the same,
while we wait for the cops. He says he wants his car right
where it is and he had the right of way 'cause he was makin'
a legal turn. So we're waitin' for the cops. Some cars go by.
The guy's car is this big fuckin' Buick. Around the corner
comes this little red Triumph. The driver's this blond kid

got this blond girl next to him. You can see what's gonna happen. There's this fuckin' car sittin' there, nobody in it. So the Triumph goes crashin' into the back of the Buick with nobody in it. BIFF-BANG-BOOM. And everything stops. We're staring. It's all still. And then that fuckin' Buick kinda shudders and starts to move. With nobody in it. It starts to roll from the impact. And it rolls just far enough to get where the road starts a downgrade. It's driftin' to the right. It's driftin' to the shoulder and over it and onto this hill, where it's pickin' up speed 'cause the hill is steep and then it disappears over the side, and into the dark, just rollin' real quiet. Rooney falls over, he's laughin' so hard. I don't know what to do. In a minute the cops come and in another minute some guy comes runnin' up over the hill to tell us some other guy had got run over by this car with nobody in it. We didn't know what to think. This was fuckin' unbelievable to us. But we found out later from the cops that this wasn't true and some guy had got hit over the head with a bottle in a bar and when he staggered out the door it was just at the instant that this fuckin' Buick with nobody in it went by. Seein' this, the guy stops cold and turns around and just goes back into the bar. Rooney is screamin' at me how we been in four goddamn accidents and fights and how we have got out clean. So then we got everything all straightened out and we come back here to play hide-and-seek 'cause that's what ole Rooney wanted.

(He is taking another drink, but finding the bottle empty.)
Only now I can't find him.

(Near RICHIE'S *footlocker stands a beer bottle and* COKES *begins to move toward it. Slowly he bends and grasps the bottle; he straightens, looking at it. He drinks. And settles down on* RICHIE'S *footlocker.)*
I'll just sit a little.

*(*RICHIE, *lying on his belly, shudders. The sobs burst out*

of him. He is shaking. COKES, *blinking, turns to study*
RICHIE.)
What's up? Hey, what're you cryin' about, soldier? Hey?
(RICHIE *cannot help himself.*)
What's he cryin' about?

ROGER (*Disgustedly, he sits there.*) He's cryin' 'cause he's a
queer.

COKES Oh. You a queer, boy?

RICHIE Yes, Sergeant.

COKES Oh.
(*Pause*)
How long you been a queer?

ROGER All his fuckin' life.

RICHIE I don't know.

COKES (*Turning to scold* ROGER) Don't be yellin' mean at him.
Boy, I tell you it's a real strange thing the way havin' leukemia gives you a lotta funny thoughts about things. Two
months ago—or maybe even yesterday—I'da called a boy
who was a queer a lotta awful names. But now I just wanna
be figurin' things out. I mean, you ain't kiddin' me out
about ole Rooney, are you, boys, 'cause of how I'm a
sergeant and you're enlisted men, so you got some idea a
vengeance on me? You ain't doin' that, are you, boys?

ROGER No.

RICHIE Ohhhh. Jesus. Ohhhh. I don't know what's hurtin'
in me.

COKES No, no, boy. You listen to me. You gonna be okay.
There's a lotta worse things in this world than bein' a queer.
I seen a lot of 'em, too. I mean, you could have leukemia.
That's worse. That can kill you. I mean, it's okay. You

listen to the ole sarge. I mean, maybe I was a queer, I wouldn't have leukemia. Who's to say? Lived a whole different life. Who's to say? I keep thinkin' there was maybe somethin' I coulda done different. Maybe not drunk so much. Or if I'd killed more gooks, or more Krauts or more dinks. I was kind-hearted sometimes. Or if I'd had a wife and I had some kids. Never had any. But my mother did and she died of it anyway. Gives you a whole funny different way a lookin' at things, I'll tell you. Ohhhhh, Rooney, Rooney.

(Slight pause)

Or if I'd let that little gook outa that spider hole he was in, I was sittin' on it. I'd let him out now, he was in there.

(He rattles the footlocker lid under him.)

Oh, how'm I ever gonna forget it? That funny little guy. I'm runnin' along, he pops up outa that hole. I'm never gonna forget him—how'm I ever gonna forget him? I see him and dive, goddamn bullet hits me in the side, I'm midair, everything's turnin' around. I go over the edge of this ditch and I'm crawlin' real fast. I lost my rifle. Can't find it. Then I come up behind him. He's half out of the hole. I bang him on top of his head, stuff him back into the hole with a grenade for company. Then I'm sittin' on the lid and it's made outa steel. I can feel him in there, though, bangin' and yellin' under me, and his yelling I can hear is begging for me to let him out. It was like a goddamn Charlie Chaplin movie, everybody fallin' down and clumsy, and him in there yellin' and bangin' away, and I'm just sittin' there lookin' around. And he was Charlie Chaplin. I don't know who I was. And then he blew up.

(Pause)

Maybe I'll just get a little shut-eye right sittin' here while I'm waitin' for ole Rooney. We figure it out. All of it. You don't mind I just doze a little here, you boys?

ROGER No.

RICHIE No.

(ROGER *rises and walks to the door. He switches off the light and gently closes the door. The transom glows.* COKES *sits in a flower of light.* ROGER *crosses back to his bunk and settles in, sitting.*)

COKES Night, boys.

RICHIE Night, Sergeant.
(COKES *sits there, fingers entwined, trying to sleep.*)

COKES I mean, he was like Charlie Chaplin. And then he
blew up.

ROGER (*Suddenly feeling very sad for this old man*) Sergeant
. . . maybe you was Charlie Chaplin, too.

COKES No. No.
(*Pause*)
No. I don't know who I was. Night.

ROGER You think he was singin' it?

COKES What?

ROGER You think he was singin' it?

COKES Oh, yeah. Oh, yeah; he was singin' it.
(*Slight pause.* COKES, *sitting on the footlocker, begins to sing a makeshift language imitating Korean, to the tune of "Beautiful Streamer." He begins with an angry, mocking energy that slowly becomes a dream, a lullaby, a farewell, a lament.*)
Yo no som lo no
Ung toe lo knee
Ra so me la lo
La see see oh doe.

Doe no tee ta ta
Too low see see
Ra mae me lo lo
Ah boo boo boo eee.
Boo boo eee booo eeee
La so lee lem
Lem lo lee da ung
Uhhh so ba booooo ohhhh.
Boo booo eee ung ba
Eee eee la looo
Lem lo lala la
Eeee oohhh ohhh ohhh ohhhhh.

(In the silence, he makes the soft, whispering sound of a child imitating an explosion, and his entwined fingers come apart. The dark figures of RICHIE and ROGER are near. The lingering light fades.)

A NOTE ON THE TYPE

This book was set on the Linotype in Electra, a type face designed by W. A. Dwiggins. The Electra face is a simple and readable type suitable for printing books by present-day processes. It is not based on any historical model, and hence does not echo any particular time or fashion.

This book was composed by The Book Press, Brattleboro, Vermont, and printed and bound by The Haddon Craftsmen, Inc., Scranton, Pennsylvania.

Display and binding design by Camilla Filancia

$10.95

"*Streamers* is absolutely a knockout! A shocking and provocative play emerging with something of the poet to it."
—Clive Barnes, *The New York Times*

"Compassion and cognition are locked together in Rabe and this fusion produces an explosive force!" —Jack Kroll, *Newsweek*

With his earlier plays—*The Basic Training of Pavlo Hummel, Sticks and Bones,* and *In the Boom Boom Room*—David Rabe established himself as one of America's leading young playwrights. *Streamers* is his most powerful and successful play.

Set in an army barracks in the early days of the Vietnam War, *Streamers* has electrified audiences from its first performance with its explosive portrayal of a handful of soldiers and their fatally inter-twined destinies . . . Richie, a wealthy neurotic who cannot resist temptation . . . Billy, an earnest midwestern straight arrow . . . Roger, a street-wise refugee from the ghetto . . . Carlyle, a pathological misfit who threatens the order and the substance of their lives . . . and Sergeants Cokes and Rooney, two aging dipsomaniacal soldiers whose grimly humorous song (about parachutes that fail to open) gives the play both its title and its fundamentally compassionate tone:

> Beautiful streamer,
> Open for me,
> The sky is above me,
> But no canopy.

Streamers is a classic of the American theater.

Illustrated with 4 pages of photographs by Martha Swope
Cover painting by Paul Davis

ALFRED A. KNOPF, PUBLISHER, NEW YORK

394-73314-2